Howl of the Dire Wolfs

Table of Contents

Introduction 1

Chapter 1 The Whispering Winds 3

    The Silent Call of the Forest 4

    A World on the Brink of Change 6

    The Arrival of the Wolf's Song 8

Chapter 2 The Ancient Prophecy 11

    The Foretelling of Doom 12

    The Seer's Vision 14

    Ancient Rites and Forgotten Lore 17

Chapter 3 The First Howl 20

    The Awakening of the Alpha 21

    A New Moon's Curse 23

    A Howl that Shakes the Earth 26

Chapter 4 Into the Wilds 29

    The Journey Begins 30

    Through the Twisted Pines 32

    Foes Lurking in the Shadows 35

Chapter 5 The Moonlit Ritual 38

    The Secret Ceremony 39

    Blood of the Pack... 42

    Under the Watchful Eyes of the Moon 44

Chapter 6 The Pack's Strength 47

    Unity in the face of adversity... 48

    The Alpha's Command 50

    Bond of Blood and Fur 53

Chapter 7 The Shattered Peace 56

    Intruders at the Gates 57

    Tensions Among Allies 60

    The Fractured Alliance 64

Chapter 8 Blood and Betrayal 69

    A Friend Turned Foe 70

    The Knife in the Back.. 74

    The Aftermath of Treachery 78

Chapter 9 The Dark Hunter 83

    The Phantom in the Night.. 84

    An Enemy Without Mercy.. 88

    Tracking the Shadows.. 92

Chapter 10 The Final Stand... 97

The Gathering Storm 98

Preparing for Battle 102

The Clash of Fangs and Steel 106

Conclusion 111

Introduction

The world of the Dire Wolves is one of ancient mysticism, untamed wilderness, and primal strength. Deep within the forests, mountains, and forgotten lands, the wolves have always been a part of the natural order. Their howls echo through the night, a haunting call that resonates with the very soul of the earth. The call is not merely a sound, but a summons an invitation to all creatures who hear it to remember their place in the grand design of nature. The wolves are not just hunters; they are protectors of the balance, ensuring the survival of the wild.

The Dire Wolves are no ordinary creatures. Larger, fiercer, and more intelligent than their common kin, they are the guardians of an ancient secret. In their blood runs the power of old magic, a connection to a forgotten age when the world was shaped by creatures of legend. Their pack is bound by unbreakable ties loyalty, trust, and survival are their cornerstones. The forest, with its dense trees and shadowed underbrush, serves as both their home and their battleground. This is a world where every decision can mean life or death, and every moonlit night holds the promise of something greater.

As the story unfolds, the Dire Wolves face a dire prophecy one that threatens to unravel their existence and the very fabric of the natural world. Forces both known and unknown will challenge their strength, loyalty, and resolve. But through the blood, betrayal, and darkness, a new dawn approaches, one that could alter the fate of the wolves and the world they protect. The howls of the Dire Wolves will not fade quietly into the night. Instead, they will rise louder, stronger, and more determined than ever before.

Chapter 1
The Whispering Winds

In the heart of an ancient forest, untouched by time, the wind carries secrets that only the wild can understand. The trees, tall and mighty, sway gently in response to the whispers that move between them. These whispers are not of the wind alone; they are the voice of the forest itself, a voice known only to those who listen closely enough to hear its true meaning. The forest, in all its wild beauty, has always known the wolves. Their presence is both feared and revered, woven into the very fabric of the land. The Silent Call of the Forest is a subtle, almost imperceptible sound that stirs within the deepest corners of the wilderness. It is a call that reverberates across the earth, an invitation to those who are brave enough to answer it.

As the world around them shifts, the creatures of the forest sense the coming storm. It is a world on the brink of change, where the balance of power between man and nature teeters precariously. Forces are at work, unseen by human eyes, that threaten to upset the ancient harmony of the wild. But the wolves, the guardians of this delicate balance, have always known that change is inevitable. They are no strangers to it. What they don't yet know, however, is that the coming change will be unlike anything they have ever faced before.

The world they protect is on the edge of transformation, and it will demand more from them than ever before.

In the quiet of the night, as the winds carry the scent of danger, the howls of the wolves rise to meet the moon. The sound echoes through the trees, a powerful reminder of the wolves' place in the world. But tonight, the howls are different. They are not simply calls to the pack; they are the Arrival of the Wolf's Song, a song that heralds a new era. The wolves' ancient song, once a symbol of strength and unity, now carries a note of urgency. Something stirs in the darkness, something that has long been forgotten, but is now returning. The wolves must rise, for the fate of the forest and the world rests on their shoulders. The Silent Call of the Forest grows louder, the winds carrying with them a message that will set in motion a series of events that none can ignore.

The Silent Call of the Forest

The Silent Call of the Forest is a sound that is both ancient and timeless. It is not a noise that can be easily heard by those who wander through the woods, but it is felt by those who are attuned to the rhythms of nature. It is a whisper carried on the wind, a murmur through the leaves, an echo of a time long past. Those who have lived in harmony with the forest, like the wolves, understand it, for it is the language of the wild.

The forest has a life of its own, and within this life is a deep and unspoken bond between the creatures that call it home. The trees, towering and rooted in the earth, stand like sentinels, their branches swaying with the wind as if listening to a distant conversation. The creatures of the forest, from the smallest insect to the mighty wolves, are all part of this conversation, though not all can understand it fully. The Silent Call of the Forest is the way the land speaks, a call that transcends words and reaches into the very soul of the forest's inhabitants.

For those who listen closely enough, the sound is present in every rustle of the leaves, in every shift of the breeze, in the subtle movements of the branches. It is the way the forest breathes, its pulse beating in time with the world. It is a call that stirs within the hearts of those who live in tune with nature, a summons to heed the warning of the earth when danger approaches. It is a feeling as much as it is a sound—an unspoken understanding that something important is unfolding.

This silent call is often heard by those who have spent years in the forest, those who know its every corner and every whisper. The wolves, with their sharp instincts and deep connection to the land, hear this call more clearly than any other creature. It is the ancient bond they share with the wilderness, a connection passed down through generations. The wolves' heightened senses allow them to feel the subtle shifts in the air, to perceive the changes in the wind, to sense when the earth is calling out to them.

The Silent Call is not always a warning of danger. Sometimes, it is a reminder of the forest's balance, of the harmony that must be maintained. It is the way the trees sway to signal the coming of a new season or the way the animals change their behavior when the time for migration approaches. It is the rhythm of life that the wolves follow, knowing when to move, when to hunt, and when to rest.

However, when the Silent Call grows louder, it is a sign that something is wrong. It may signal the arrival of a new threat, one that disrupts the delicate balance the wolves and other creatures have worked so hard to protect. The winds may carry a different scent, the trees may seem to whisper in alarm, and the ground beneath their paws may feel unsettled. When this happens, the wolves know they must act quickly. The forest is calling out for them to protect it, to restore the balance that has been disrupted.

The Silent Call of the Forest is not just a sound; it is a reminder that the land is alive and that everything within it is interconnected. The wolves understand this better than most. Their survival depends not only on their strength and cunning but on their ability to listen to the forest, to understand its silent language, and to respond when it calls.

A World on the Brink of Change

A World on the Brink of Change is a concept that encapsulates the delicate moment before a pivotal transformation. It is a time when everything, from the smallest creature to the largest mountain, is poised for something that will alter the fabric of existence. In this world, nothing remains static; the winds of change are constantly shifting, whispering of a new dawn, a new challenge, or a new threat. The environment, once harmonious and predictable, now feels like an unsettled force, and the signs are everywhere, if one knows how to look.

For centuries, the natural world has been governed by the steady rhythms of life seasons that come and go, cycles of birth and death, and patterns that repeat without fail. But even the most stable systems are not immune to change. In the forest, the once-peaceful coexistence between creatures is beginning to fracture. The air, once crisp and clear, now carries a sense of tension, as if the earth itself senses an impending upheaval. The trees stand tall and silent, their ancient roots grounded deep in the earth, yet even they seem to tremble, whispering of things to come. The animals, too, feel the shift some grow restless, others retreat into the shadows, and a few instinctively understand that a great storm is brewing just beyond the horizon.

This world on the brink of change is not just a physical one, but an emotional and spiritual one as well. The wolves, the guardians of the forest, have always been in tune with the pulse of nature, and they sense that the harmony of the world they have known for so long is starting to unravel. The pack, once unified and steadfast, begins to feel the strain of unknown forces pulling at its very core. The bonds between the members of the pack, forged over generations, begin to weaken under the pressure of unseen threats. It is as if the very earth beneath them is stirring, preparing for something vast and unpredictable. The wolves, wise in their ways, understand that the land they protect is no longer the sanctuary it once was. They must adapt, evolve, and face the storm that looms on the horizon, for the world they know is about to change in ways they could never have imagined.

The human world, too, is on the edge of transformation. In the distance, the faint hum of civilization grows louder new technologies, new ideologies, and new conflicts are beginning to seep into the wilderness. The balance between man and nature, once a careful equilibrium, is tipping, and the consequences of this shift are not yet fully understood. The wolves, and all the creatures of the forest, feel the encroachment of these forces. The forests, once an impenetrable barrier between human and nature, are being cleared, tamed, and controlled. Cities are expanding, and the wild places that once seemed safe from the reach of mankind are now under threat. The wolves' sanctuary is no longer invulnerable, and they must adapt to the changing world or risk losing everything they have fought to protect.

In this moment of flux, the creatures of the forest are faced with a choice: to remain stagnant, holding on to the old ways, or to embrace the inevitable changes that are sweeping across the land. They must find a new path forward, one that allows them to thrive in a world that is rapidly shifting. For the wolves, this is not just a physical battle; it is a battle for their place in the world, for the future of their pack, and for the survival of the natural order. The world on the brink of change is a world of uncertainty, but it is also a world full of possibility a world where new alliances can be forged, new strengths can be discovered, and new legends can be born. How the wolves respond to this moment will determine the course of their future and the future of the land they call home.

The Arrival of the Wolf's Song

The Arrival of the Wolf's Song marks a pivotal moment in the forest, a moment when the wolves' ancient call echoes through the trees and into the hearts of all who hear it. It is a sound that has been passed down through generations, carried on the wind like a legacy from the past, but its arrival is always felt in the present. When the wolves sing, it is not just an ordinary howl; it is a powerful declaration that something significant is unfolding. The song of the wolf is a primal cry that resonates with both the wild and the untamed spirit within every creature of the forest.

For the wolves, their song is a connection to something far older than their own lives. It is a reminder of the bond they share with the land and the rhythm of the world they protect. The wolves' song is not merely a vocalization, but a language in itself — a language that speaks to the heart of the forest, calling upon the spirits of the earth, sky, and water. It is an invitation for the pack to unite, to come together in the face of an unknown challenge or opportunity, to prepare for what lies ahead.

When the wolves begin to sing, it is often at the cusp of a change, when the air grows thick with the sense that something is about to shift. The wind carries the sound through the forest, reaching the ears of creatures both large and small. For some, it is a warning—a sign that the balance of nature is in jeopardy. For others, it is a call to action, a summons to gather and prepare for the challenges that await. The arrival of the wolf's song does not just stir the wolves themselves; it awakens the very soul of the forest. The trees seem to sway in rhythm, the leaves rustling as if answering the call, and the earth beneath their paws hums with the energy of the forest's ancient power.

The wolves' song carries with it a sense of urgency, as if the pack is called to rise to something greater than itself. It is a call for unity, a reminder that strength lies in the bond between members of the pack. When the song fills the air, it spreads across the land like wildfire, igniting the spirits of the creatures who hear it. Each howl carries with it the weight of a thousand years of history, of battles fought and victories won, and of the relentless survival of the pack. The song serves as a reminder of the wolves' role as guardians, protectors of the forest and its ancient secrets. It is a declaration of strength, resilience, and unity in the face of adversity.

But as the song carries through the night, there is an undertone of something deepera sense of the unknown. The wolves do not sing for nothing. Their song is a signal, a beacon that something is on the horizon. The world they know is about to change, and the wolves are being called to play their part in whatever comes next. As the howl echoes through the forest, it becomes clear that the pack must brace itself for a challenge unlike any it has faced before. The song of the wolves is not just a cry for unity; it is a call to arms, a summons to rise and meet the future head-on. The arrival of the wolf's song marks the beginning of a new chapter in their journey, one that will test their strength, their loyalty, and their connection to the land they protect.

Chapter 2
The Ancient Prophecy

Long before the wolves' first howl echoed through the forest, the land was ruled by ancient forces whose power extended far beyond the reach of ordinary creatures. In those early days, the world was shaped by the whispers of prophecies, spoken by those who could peer into the future and see the threads of destiny woven together. Among them was the Seer, a mysterious figure who had long lived in the shadows of time. It was the Seer who first spoke of the doom that loomed on the horizon, a darkness that threatened to engulf the land and disrupt the delicate balance between nature and civilization. The foretelling was not a simple warning; it was a solemn declaration that a great calamity was approaching, one that could undo all that had been built by the creatures of the forest.

The Seer's vision was sharp, unclouded by doubt or fear, and it painted a picture of a world in turmoil. From the depths of the forest to the farthest reaches of the mountains, the prophecy spoke of a time when the wolves would be tested beyond their limits. The doom that was foretold would not come in the form of a single enemy but would take many shapes, from the encroachment of man to the rise of ancient beings long thought to be myths. The Seer saw the wolves in the center of it all, their fates intertwined with the survival of the world itself. The prophecy spoke of the wolves' role as the last line of defense against the coming storm, a storm that would test their loyalty, their strength, and their very existence.

As the years passed, the prophecy was passed down through the generations, becoming more than just a warning. It became a part of the wolves' very identity, shaping their understanding of their place in the world. The ancient rites, once performed by the Seer to channel the power of the earth, became rituals of preparation, a way to connect with the land and harness its strength in times of need. But as the years turned into centuries, much of the lore surrounding the prophecy was lost. The wolves continued to live their lives, unaware that the moment of reckoning was drawing ever closer. What had once been a tale of doom and survival was now little more than a forgotten legend, buried beneath the weight of time and the changing world.

Yet, the signs were there, hidden in the winds and carried in the whispers of the forest. The prophecy was not just a tale to be forgotten; it was a call to action, waiting for the right moment to be remembered. The ancient rites, though lost, had left their mark on the wolves, and the forgotten lore would resurface when the pack needed it most. The time of reckoning had arrived, and the wolves were about to face the truth of the Seer's vision. The world they had known was about to change, and the prophecy would no longer be a distant memory. It was time to act.

The Foretelling of Doom

The Foretelling of Doom was not a simple tale of disaster passed down through the generations; it was a warning imbued with both dread and purpose. For centuries, the prophecy had been spoken in hushed tones, its words echoed through the forests and caves, carried by the wind from the elders to the young, who listened in awe and fear. It was said that the first Seer, an ancient being with the ability to commune with the land itself, had glimpsed the dark future that awaited the world. The Seer's vision, sharpened by years of wisdom, was both vivid and horrifying a vision of the balance between nature and the world being violently upturned, leaving the creatures of the forest vulnerable to destruction.

The prophecy foretold that the land, once thriving with life and harmony, would face a dark awakening. Forces beyond the comprehension of the forest's creatures were brewing, pushing against the natural order with an unstoppable force. What was once a peaceful world, governed by cycles of growth and decay, would soon find itself under siege, as enemies both known and unknown began to encroach upon the wilderness. This doom was not a single event or battle; it was a gradual erosion, a slow-burning destruction that would engulf the land. The Seer's warning was precise in its message the wolves, the guardians of the forest, would be caught in the heart of this chaos.

The Foretelling of Doom spoke of a time when the wolves would be tested like never before. It described a shadow that would grow larger and darker, casting its reach across the land. This darkness was not only a force that could be seen, but also something that would twist the very essence of the forest, corrupting its purity. The balance that had sustained the creatures for generations would be shattered, and the natural forces would be thrown into disarray. The wolves would be the first to feel the shift, for they were the keepers of the forest's heart. Their strength, intelligence, and unity would be the key to survival, but even they were not immune to the forces at work.

The prophecy spoke of strange and unnatural creatures rising from forgotten places, beings that had long slumbered in the depths of the earth, awakened by the disturbance in the balance. The Seer saw them clearly large, formidable, and hungry for power. These creatures, once thought to be mere myth, would be unleashed upon the world, their only goal to dominate and destroy. As the wolves prepared to face these new threats, the prophecy revealed that the forest itself would no longer be the sanctuary it once was. The wolves would no longer be able to rely solely on their instincts; they would have to face challenges that were far beyond their comprehension, battles that required not just strength, but wisdom and sacrifice.

The doom that was foretold was not a sudden storm or a brief skirmish; it was a gradual descent into chaos, a world that would be forever altered. The Seer's vision painted a picture of a time when the wolves would find themselves caught between the old world and the new, between the forces of nature and the encroaching threat of destruction. The Foretelling of Doom was not simply a tale of fear, but a call to action a reminder that even in the darkest of times, hope could be found in unity, strength, and the unbreakable bond of the pack. The wolves must face this doom together, or risk losing everything they held dear.

The Seer's Vision

The Seer's Vision was not a single image, but a tapestry of vivid and often unsettling scenes that unfolded in the mind of the ancient seer. It was a vision so powerful and clear that it seemed to transcend time itself, as if the boundaries between the past, present, and future had dissolved in an instant. The Seer, a figure revered for their connection to the earth and the spirits of the land, was granted the rare ability to see beyond the veil of ordinary sight. Their visions were not ordinary dreams; they were glimpses into the threads of destiny, a divine insight into the forces that shaped the world and the fates of those within it.

The vision began with an ominous stillness, a silence that hung heavily in the air. It was a silence that stretched across the forest, the mountains, and the rivers. For a moment, it felt as though the very heartbeat of the land had stopped. The Seer saw a land once full of life now plagued by an unsettling quiet. The usual sounds of rustling leaves, chirping birds, and the howls of wolves were absent. In their place, there was only a heavy, oppressive silence. The balance that had long existed between nature and the creatures of the earth was disrupted. This stillness was not a moment of peace but a harbinger of something far worse a sign that something malevolent was beginning to take shape in the shadows.

From this silence, the Seer saw a dark figure begin to emerge. At first, it was merely a shadow, a silhouette against the dimming light of the forest. But as it drew closer, the figure began to take form, revealing a creature unlike anything the Seer had ever seen. It was monstrous, towering above the trees, with eyes that glowed like embers in the night. Its movements were slow, deliberate, and filled with an unnatural power. The Seer could sense that this creature was not alone; it was part of something larger, a force that had been dormant for centuries but was now awakening. This figure represented the coming storm, a force of destruction that would tear through the forest and the lives of its creatures.

As the Seer's vision deepened, the shadowy figure began to grow in number, multiplying into an army of dark beings, each one more grotesque than the last. They were not of flesh and bone, but something darker, more insidious a manifestation of the world's impending decay. These beings were drawn to the heart of the forest, to the place where the wolves' pack had long stood as guardians. The wolves, who had always been the protectors of the land, would now be faced with an enemy unlike any they had ever known. These dark entities were not just creatures of violence; they were embodiments of chaos itself, bent on unraveling the very fabric of existence.

The Seer then saw the wolves, not as mere creatures of instinct, but as symbols of hope and strength. The pack would face these shadows, but they would not do so alone. The vision showed a gathering of unlikely allies creatures from all corners of the forest, from the smallest insects to the grandest of the trees coming together to stand against the encroaching darkness. The Seer saw the wolves, united as never before, their strength and unity being their greatest weapon. The vision was clear: the pack must face this doom together, relying not only on their strength but also on their wisdom and their ability to trust each other.

In the final moments of the vision, the Seer saw a flicker of light breaking through the darkness. The wolves, bloodied and weary, stood tall in the face of the storm, their howls echoing through the night. It was not the end, but a beginning the beginning of a battle that would determine the fate of the forest, the wolves, and the very world they inhabited. The Seer's vision ended with a single, powerful image: the wolves, standing together in the face of the coming darkness, their song rising as a defiant challenge to the forces that sought to destroy them.

This vision, once a private glimpse into the future, became a guiding force for the wolves. The Seer had shown them what was to come, and it was now up to them to fulfill their role in the prophecy. The time for preparation was over. The battle had already begun.

Ancient Rites and Forgotten Lore

The ancient rites and forgotten lore of the wolves were steeped in the history of their kind, passed down through generations, wrapped in the mystery of ages long past. These rituals, once a fundamental part of their existence, had been practiced since the dawn of their lineage. Each rite held a deep meaning, a purpose beyond what could be seen with the eyes, and each carried with it the weight of a world that had lived in harmony with the earth for millennia. Over time, much of the lore surrounding these rituals was lost, fading into the whispers of the wind and the shadows of the forest. Yet, some fragments remained tales, gestures, and symbols that still held the power to bind the wolves to the ancient forces of nature.

The rites were not mere ceremonies; they were ways of honoring the land, the ancestors, and the spirits that protected the forest. Every season, every moon cycle, the wolves would gather to perform rituals that ensured the survival and prosperity of their pack. These rites were often conducted in sacred places deep within the forest groves where the trees stood tall and ancient, places where the energy of the earth felt strongest. There, the wolves would come together, united by their shared purpose, to perform acts that strengthened their bond with the land and reaffirmed their role as guardians of the wild.

One of the most important rites was the *Moonrise Ceremony*, held on the night of the full moon. It was a time when the wolves would come together to pay homage to the moon, which was considered a symbol of strength and unity. The ceremony began with a silent procession to the heart of the forest, where the pack would circle beneath the moonlight, their eyes fixed on the sky. The Alpha would then lead the pack in a chorus of howls, each one rising in pitch and power until it reverberated through the entire forest. This was no ordinary howl, but a sound that reached deep into the earth, connecting the wolves to the ancient power that flowed through the land. The howls were a prayer, a call to the spirits of the earth and the ancestors who had long since passed, asking for their guidance and protection.

Another important ritual was the *Spirit Hunt*, which took place when the pack was in need of guidance or direction. This ritual was not a hunt for food but a hunt for the spirit of the land. The wolves would venture deep into the forest, seeking the presence of the sacred creatures that roamed there beasts that were believed to carry the wisdom of the earth in their blood. These creatures, often unseen by human eyes, would guide the pack to the answers they sought. The Spirit Hunt was a time of reflection and connection, allowing the wolves to align themselves with the forces that governed their world. It was said that those who completed the Spirit Hunt with a pure heart would be granted the wisdom to face any challenge that lay ahead.

The forgotten lore, too, was filled with stories and teachings that had been passed down from the wolves' ancestors. These tales were rich with metaphor and meaning, often recounting the origins of the pack, the trials they had faced, and the victories they had won. One such story told of the first Alpha, a wolf who had learned the language of the earth and had forged a bond with the spirits of the land. This Alpha, according to the lore, had been the one to first teach the wolves the ancient rites, ensuring that their bond with nature would be unbroken. These stories, though often shrouded in myth, held truths that the wolves needed to remember. They were the foundation of their existence, a reminder of their purpose and the sacred duty they held to the forest.

As time passed, much of this knowledge faded, hidden in the shadows of the forest and the recesses of memory. But when the winds began to change, when the foretelling of doom became undeniable, the wolves realized that the ancient rites and forgotten lore were no longer relics of the past. They were keys to survival, tools that could help them face the challenges that awaited them. The wisdom of their ancestors was not lost; it was merely waiting to be rediscovered. And so, the wolves began to seek out the forgotten places, the ancient groves and sacred sites, to reconnect with the land and the rites that had once protected them. Only by embracing the past could they hope to face the future. The ancient rites and forgotten lore had not lost their power; they were the wolves' only hope for surviving the darkness that was about to descend upon them.

Chapter 3
The First Howl

The First Howl marked the beginning of a new chapter in the world of the wolves, a moment that would forever alter the course of their destiny. It was a sound that resonated through the forest, carrying with it a power that could not be ignored. The air was thick with tension, and the usual sounds of the wild seemed muted, as if the very earth itself was holding its breath. The forest, for all its age and wisdom, had never felt quite like this before. Something was stirring deep within it, something ancient and untamed. The wolves could feel it, and at the center of it all stood the Alpha, whose awakening was not just a physical moment but the unlocking of an ancient power that had long been dormant.

The Alpha, a leader whose strength was forged in the heart of the wilderness, had always carried the weight of the pack's survival on their shoulders. But with the First Howl, something shifted. It was as if the very blood of the Alpha had been ignited, awakening a force that had been dormant for generations. This was no ordinary moment of leadership; it was the spark that would ignite the flames of change. The forest seemed to respond to the Alpha's awakening, the trees swaying in anticipation, the wind howling as if it, too, could sense the importance of what was unfolding. The Alpha, once a figure of strength and guidance, now carried the weight of an entire world in their howl.

But with the Alpha's awakening came a curse, one that would be tied to the new moon that rose on that fateful night. The curse was not one of malice, but of inevitability. The wolves had always understood the balance of nature the moon, the seasons, the flow of life. But the new moon that night brought with it a disruption, a force that threatened to unravel the very fabric of their existence. The curse was one of prophecy, a warning that the wolves' time of peace was coming to an end. The Alpha, now awakened, could feel the weight of this curse, a burden that would shape their leadership in ways they had never anticipated.

The First Howl, as it echoed through the trees, was not just a cry of power, but one of desperation. The sound shook the earth itself, reverberating through the very bones of the forest. It was a howl that carried with it the urgency of the pack's survival, a call to arms that could not be ignored. The earth trembled with the force of the Alpha's cry, and the pack knew that the time for inaction was over. The First Howl had set in motion a chain of events that would test their strength, their loyalty, and their very essence. The wolves had awoken to a world on the brink of destruction, and their howl would be the sound of defiance against the coming storm.

The Awakening of the Alpha

The Awakening of the Alpha was a moment long anticipated, yet shrouded in mystery. It was said that the Alpha would rise not simply through time or by bloodline, but through an ancient force that called to them from the depths of the forest and the very soul of the earth. It was a power that could not be denied, a connection so deep that it transcended the limits of natural understanding. For the wolves, the Alpha was not just a leader. They were the embodiment of the pack's strength, its spirit, and its very survival. The awakening of the Alpha was not just the beginning of their reign. It was the moment when the very fabric of the pack and the forest would shift, when the destinies of all would be forever altered.

For years, the forest had been quiet. The pack, though strong and united, had not felt the urgency of change. But in the darkness of the night, as the winds shifted and the trees whispered of things yet unseen, something stirred deep within the heart of the Alpha. It was as if a hidden force had finally decided that the time had come, a force that had lain dormant for generations, waiting for the right moment to awaken. The call was not heard with ears, but with an instinct so powerful that it surged through the Alpha's veins, igniting a fire that had long been suppressed.

The Alpha's awakening was a sudden event, but it felt inevitable in its unfolding. There was no grand ceremony or dramatic declaration. It began with a single, subtle change. The air around the Alpha grew still, the sounds of the forest muffled, as though the world itself had paused to bear witness. The Alpha, once a figure of quiet authority, now stood taller, their body infused with a new energy. Their eyes, once calm and observant, burned with an intensity that seemed to pierce through the very darkness around them. The wolves in the pack could feel it, the palpable shift in the air, the sense that something extraordinary was happening.

The ground beneath the Alpha's paws seemed to hum with life, vibrating with a power that could not be contained. The trees, ancient and towering, bent slightly toward them, as if acknowledging their rise. It was as though the Alpha had tapped into something far older than the pack itself, a force older than the forest, older than the world they had known. In that moment, the Alpha was no longer just a leader by virtue of bloodline or strength. They were something more, something primal, something that the land itself had chosen to awaken.

The Awakening of the Alpha was also the awakening of the pack's true potential. It was a moment of realization for the wolves. They understood now that the Alpha was not simply a guide but the key to their survival. The pack's unity was tied to the Alpha's strength. The bond between them was woven together with the Alpha at its center, and now, with the Alpha's awakening, this bond would be tested like never before. The pack would have to rise to meet the challenges ahead, challenges they could not face alone. The Alpha's awakening called not just for leadership, but for unity, loyalty, and a strength that transcended their individual abilities.

As the Alpha stood, surrounded by the pack, their gaze swept across the wolves. In their eyes burned not just the fire of their newfound power, but the weight of the coming storm. The Awakening of the Alpha was more than the rise of a leader. It was the beginning of a battle for survival, a battle that would change the pack's fate forever. The call had been answered, and now the wolves were ready to face what lay ahead, together.

A New Moon's Curse

A New Moon's Curse was a dark omen, a mysterious and foreboding event that loomed over the wolves like a shadow, its presence subtle yet undeniable. Unlike the full moon, which bathed the forest in silver light and stirred the wolves' primal instincts to hunt and howl, the new moon was a time of darkness—a time when the very essence of the land seemed to hold its breath. It was during this moonless night that the curse would be unleashed, a force so ancient and powerful that it threatened to unravel the fabric of the natural world.

The curse itself was not born of any one individual, but from a deep and ancient well of magic that existed long before the wolves roamed the forest. It was a magic tied to the very balance of the world, a force that maintained harmony between the creatures of the earth and the unseen spirits that guided them. But the new moon, in its silent rise, marked a time when this balance would falter. The wolves, though powerful and in tune with the rhythms of nature, could not escape the pull of this dark force. It was as though the land itself had been corrupted, and with the arrival of the new moon, the curse was set into motion, stirring deep within the earth.

The curse was not an instant event, but a gradual change that crept into the lives of the wolves, altering the very fabric of their existence. The first sign was subtle an unnatural stillness that settled over the forest. The usual sounds of life, the rustling of leaves, the calls of birds, and the scurry of smaller creatures, all seemed to vanish. The wind, once a gentle whisper, became heavy and oppressive, as though the air itself had thickened with an unseen weight. The wolves felt it in their bones, this sudden change in the environment, but they could not yet understand its true meaning.

The new moon's curse had begun to manifest in strange and disturbing ways. The wolves' once sharp instincts dulled, their senses clouded by an overwhelming sense of confusion. The usual clarity of the pack's unity began to waver. The Alpha, the once-unshakable leader, felt the weight of the curse most acutely. Their connection to the land, once so strong, seemed to fray at the edges, as if the very earth beneath them was slipping away. The Alpha's strength, once fueled by the ancient magic of the forest, was now tempered by a sense of dread. They could feel the curse's influence creeping into their every decision, clouding their judgment, and disrupting their once unbreakable connection to their pack.

The curse was not just a physical affliction but a spiritual one as well. The wolves, deeply connected to the land and its spirits, found themselves estranged from the natural world. Their once harmonious bond with the forest began to deteriorate. The trees, once their silent guardians, now seemed distant, their branches no longer offering protection. The spirits of the forest, which had long guided the pack, became silent, their whispers lost in the heavy darkness that accompanied the new moon.

As the days passed, the curse grew stronger, affecting not just the Alpha but the entire pack. Fear began to creep into their hearts, doubt into their minds. The unity that had once defined the wolves seemed to crumble, as the curse set its grip upon them, sowing seeds of distrust and division. The pack, once a symbol of strength and unity, was now fractured, vulnerable to forces they could not comprehend.

It was clear that the curse would not lift on its own. The wolves would need to find a way to break the bond the new moon had forged with their land, to restore the balance that had been shattered. But to do so, they would need to confront the dark forces that sought to take hold of their world, to face the shadow that had been cast over their very existence. The new moon's curse was not just an affliction to be endured; it was a battle to be fought, one that would test the wolves' strength, unity, and will to survive. The pack could no longer wait for the curse to lift. They had to rise against it, to reclaim the land, their power, and their place in the world.

A Howl that Shakes the Earth

A Howl that Shakes the Earth was a moment so powerful and so charged with energy that it could be felt deep in the bones of the earth itself. It was not just a cry into the night, a call of the wolves, but a primal roar that resonated with the very forces of nature. This howl was the Alpha's cry, a symbol of both leadership and defiance. It echoed across the forest, rattling the trees and stirring the ancient spirits that inhabited the land. It was a sound so full of power, filled with the raw essence of the wild, that it could not be ignored. It was the moment the earth itself responded, shaking under the force of the Alpha's determination.

The howl did not come from a place of calm or quiet. It was born of the rising tension that had gripped the pack, a tension that had been building ever since the awakening of the Alpha. The pack, once unified and certain, now found themselves on the edge of uncertainty. The world they knew had begun to change, and the forces that sought to disrupt the delicate balance between the creatures of the forest were now closing in. The Alpha, aware of the magnitude of the coming storm, felt the weight of responsibility more heavily than ever before. The time for passive waiting was over. It was time to act, to reclaim their strength, and to face the looming darkness head-on.

The first sign of the coming howl was the stillness that fell over the pack. There was a palpable sense of anticipation, a moment when everything seemed to hold its breath. The wind stilled, the trees paused in their swaying, and the usual sounds of the forest faded into silence. In that moment, all eyes were on the Alpha. The pack knew that something monumental was about to unfold. The Alpha's body tensed, their gaze focused, and their mind clear. They could feel the energy of the earth beneath their paws, the weight of history in their chest, and the strength of the forest flowing through their veins. The pack was ready, but they needed a signal, something to bind them together in this moment of crisis.

And then, the Alpha let out a single, thunderous howl. It was a sound that reverberated through the very ground, shaking the earth and the trees around them. It was a howl that carried the weight of the past, the struggles of the pack, and the future they were about to face. It was a cry of defiance, a challenge to the darkness that was closing in on them, and a call to arms for the pack. The sound rose higher and higher, a mighty crescendo that seemed to echo through the heavens themselves. It was a howl that would be heard not just by the pack, but by every creature within earshot, a reminder that the wolves were not to be underestimated.

The howl was not just a declaration; it was a rallying cry. As the sound filled the air, the wolves felt the energy surge through them. The unity that had been shaken by the new moon's curse was reignited by the Alpha's call. The pack began to stir, their spirits rising as the call resonated within them. It was as though the very earth beneath them responded, sending waves of strength and determination through their paws, their hearts, and their minds. They were not alone. The land, the forest, and the spirits of the earth were with them. Together, they would stand against whatever forces sought to tear them apart.

The Howl that Shakes the Earth was not just a moment of power. It was a rebirth. It marked the moment when the pack rediscovered their true strength, their unity, and their purpose. The Alpha's cry, so full of energy and determination, became the symbol of what was to come—a battle to protect the land they had sworn to guard, a fight to preserve the balance of nature, and a testament to the wolves' resilience. It was the sound of their defiance, the sound of a pack that would not go down without a fight. The earth trembled beneath them, but the wolves stood tall, their spirits unbroken, ready to face the storm that was coming.

Chapter 4
Into the Wilds

The journey into the wilds was not one that the pack took lightly. It was a venture into the heart of the unknown, a place where the rules of their world no longer seemed to apply. The forest, once a familiar refuge, had become a place of mystery and danger. As the pack set out, they could feel the weight of the land pressing in on them. Every step forward felt as though it was taking them deeper into a world that was both ancient and unpredictable, where the very air seemed charged with the energy of untold secrets. The journey was not just a physical one; it was a test of their endurance, their unity, and their will to survive.

As they moved deeper into the wilderness, the path grew narrower, the trees thicker, and the shadows longer. The twisted pines that surrounded them seemed to grow in unnatural shapes, their gnarled branches reaching out like fingers, pulling at the very fabric of the pack's resolve. The forest was alive in ways they had never experienced before, its presence felt in every rustle of leaves, every snap of a twig, and the eerie silence that seemed to fall over them when they least expected it. There was a tension in the air, a sense of something waiting just beyond their reach. It was a place where even the wolves' keen instincts seemed dulled by the oppressive atmosphere, and every movement felt like a whisper against the vastness of the wilderness.

But the wilds were not just a land of silence and shadows. They were a land filled with threats lurking just out of sight. The pack knew that the deeper they ventured, the more dangerous the world around them became. The wolves had always been the predators, the rulers of the forest, but here, in the heart of the wilds, they were not the only ones. Foes, both known and unknown, moved in the shadows, watching, waiting for the perfect moment to strike. The pack's strength, unity, and resourcefulness would be tested as they faced challenges they had never imagined, enemies that would push them to their limits.

This journey would take them to the edge of their existence, to the very heart of the wilderness where survival was no longer guaranteed. The pack knew that only by staying together, by trusting each other, and by embracing the dangers of the wilds, could they hope to find their way through the darkness. The journey had begun, and there was no turning back. What lay ahead was a mystery, but the pack's resolve was unwavering. They would face whatever came their way, with courage, loyalty, and the strength of the wilds themselves.

The Journey Begins

The journey began on an early morning when the first rays of sunlight filtered through the trees, casting long shadows on the forest floor. The air was crisp, charged with the scent of damp earth and the promise of adventure. The pack, gathered at the forest's edge, stood still for a moment, as though waiting for the land itself to give them permission to step forward. There was a quiet understanding between the wolves; they all knew that this journey would change them forever. The path ahead was uncertain, fraught with dangers they could not yet see, but it was a path they had to take. There was no turning back.

The Alpha, standing at the front of the pack, took a deep breath. Their senses were heightened, attuned to the faintest whisper of the wind, the rustle of leaves, and the heartbeat of the land beneath their paws. They could feel the weight of the decision, the responsibility that had been placed on their shoulders. This was no longer just about protecting the pack. It was about survival in a world that was shifting, a world where the very rules of nature were beginning to falter. The new moon's curse had cast a shadow over their existence, and they knew that to overcome it, they had to journey into the unknown, into the wilds where no wolf had ventured in generations.

With a decisive nod, the Alpha signaled for the pack to move forward. Slowly, they began their trek into the heart of the wilds, their paws soft against the earth as they made their way through the underbrush. The forest, once a familiar home, now felt foreign, almost alive with an energy they had never sensed before. The trees stood taller, their limbs twisted into strange, unsettling shapes. The dense canopy above blocked out much of the sunlight, casting the forest floor in an eerie twilight. The air grew thicker, heavier with the scent of decay and dampness, a stark reminder that this was no longer the safe haven they had known.

The pack moved cautiously, their eyes scanning the shadows and their ears pricked for any sign of danger. Every step was measured, deliberate, as they made their way through the winding paths of the wilderness. The Alpha led with a quiet confidence, but even they could not shake the feeling that the forest was watching, waiting. Something was different here, something they could not quite grasp, but it was palpable in the very air they breathed. The wolves' instincts told them they were being tested, and every passing moment brought them closer to whatever lay ahead.

They passed through dense thickets of brambles that clawed at their fur, crossed rocky streams that rushed with cold water, and navigated around fallen trees that seemed to have grown strangely twisted with age. The path became harder to follow, the familiar trails of their ancestors now lost in the vastness of the wilds. The pack could feel the isolation, the separation from the world they had once known. The sounds of the forest were quieter here, muted by the thick underbrush and the unsettling stillness that hung over the land.

Though the wolves moved in silence, a bond stronger than ever held them together. They could feel the weight of their purpose. The pack was not just journeying through the wilds; they were venturing into the unknown in search of something greater answers, strength, and survival. The Alpha, feeling the gravity of their role, knew that each step they took was one toward the unknown, and whatever awaited them would shape their destiny. The journey had truly begun, and they would face it together, with unity and resolve, no matter what dangers the wilds held.

Through the Twisted Pines

Through the Twisted Pines, the path grew ever more treacherous. The dense forest, which had once been a welcoming refuge, now seemed to shift into something darker, more ominous. The towering pines, ancient and gnarled, bent in unnatural angles, their trunks twisted in spirals that seemed to defy the laws of nature. Their limbs stretched out like skeletal arms, reaching for the wolves as they passed beneath. The air felt thick here, charged with an energy that made the wolves' fur stand on end. It was as if the very trees were alive, watching their every move, their twisted forms reflecting the distortion of the world around them.

The pack pressed forward, their paws soft against the carpet of pine needles that blanketed the forest floor. Every step seemed to echo, amplified by the silence that surrounded them. The wind that had once whispered through the leaves now howled between the trees, a mournful sound that sent shivers through the wolves' spines. The usual comfort of the forest had faded, replaced by a sense of unease. The pines, their bark rough and marked by age, seemed to close in around them as they ventured deeper into the heart of the wilds. It was a place where shadows danced, where the light never seemed to reach the ground, and where every creaking branch or rustling leaf felt like a warning.

The Alpha led the pack with steady steps, their eyes scanning the twisted landscape ahead. Their senses were heightened, but even the sharpest instincts couldn't shake the feeling that they were being drawn into a labyrinth with no way out. The further they traveled, the harder it became to see the way forward. The trees grew closer together, their branches interlocking above to form a nearly impenetrable canopy, blocking out the sky. The path narrowed, and the pack had to maneuver carefully around the gnarled roots and thick underbrush that seemed to reach out like claws. The ground was uneven, and each step had to be calculated, ensuring that they wouldn't stumble into the hidden pitfalls of the forest.

Despite the challenges, the pack moved as one, their bond of unity stronger than ever. The wolves communicated with subtle gestures an ear flicked in one direction, a shift of weight and continued to follow their Alpha through the tangled wilderness. The journey was demanding, but there was no turning back now. The Twisted Pines seemed endless, as if the path stretched on forever, each turn and bend leading to more confusion and mystery. Yet the wolves pressed forward, their instincts guiding them through the maze of ancient trees.

As they moved deeper into the pines, strange sounds began to emerge from the shadows. The quiet rustle of the wind was joined by faint whispers, like voices carried on the breeze. But when the wolves stopped to listen, they heard nothing but the howling wind. It was as if the forest itself was speaking to them, but in a language they could not understand. The pack moved faster now, urgency driving them forward, the unease of the forest growing with each passing step.

Through the Twisted Pines, the pack realized that the forest was not just a barrier between them and their destination. It was a living, breathing entity one that was testing them, challenging their resolve. It had once been a sanctuary, a place where they had felt safe, but now, it had become something more something dangerous, a force that was pushing them to the brink of their limits. And yet, the pack did not falter. They knew that beyond these twisted trees lay the answers they sought, the path that would lead them to whatever awaited them in the depths of the wilds.

Foes Lurking in the Shadows

As the wolves pressed on through the twisting, darkened forest, an unsettling sensation began to creep over them. The further they ventured into the wilds, the more they became aware of the eyes watching them from the shadows. At first, it was only a fleeting feeling, a brush of instinct that told them they were not alone. But as the hours passed and the trees grew thicker, the sense of being hunted intensified. The wolves' keen senses told them that danger was near, lurking just beyond the flickering edges of the forest, hidden in the gloom of the twisted pines.

The pack moved cautiously, their bodies tense, every footfall silent against the forest floor. The Alpha, always attuned to the smallest disturbances in the air, slowed their pace, their ears pricked and nostrils flaring as they scanned the darkness ahead. Their sharp eyes caught every movement, every flicker of light, every shifting shadow. Yet, despite their heightened awareness, nothing emerged from the trees. The silence grew heavier, broken only by the occasional creak of a distant branch, a subtle shift in the wind, or the faintest rustle of leaves. It was the kind of quiet that made the air feel charged, as if it was only the calm before the storm.

The wolves could feel it now the tension building in the air like a storm about to break. Something was waiting for them, hiding in the shadows, its presence growing more palpable with every passing minute. The pack's instincts, honed over countless hunts, were screaming at them to remain alert. They knew the forest well, but this was different. The wilds had never felt so hostile. It wasn't the environment they feared it was what lay within it. They could sense eyes upon them, cold and predatory, watching, waiting for the perfect moment to strike.

Then, without warning, the first movement broke the stillness. A dark shape darted between the trees, its eyes glowing faintly in the dim light. It was too quick to be fully seen, a shadow that slipped in and out of sight like a wisp of smoke. The wolves froze, their bodies coiled with tension, every muscle prepared to spring into action. The Alpha's ears twitched. Their sharp gaze locked on the shape, but it was gone before they could fully focus. Another flicker of movement this time closer followed by a low, menacing growl that rumbled from the depths of the forest.

The pack's hackles rose in unison. They had been found, and they were not alone. The wolves' senses told them they were surrounded, though they couldn't see their attackers. The presence of something dark and powerful pressed in from all sides. The pack began to form a protective circle, their instincts guiding them to stay close and defend their vulnerable members. The Alpha growled softly, signaling the pack to prepare for battle. They could feel the weight of the moment, the air thick with the promise of confrontation. Whatever lurked in the shadows, they were about to face it.

The dark shapes finally revealed themselves. From behind the twisted trunks of the pines, strange creatures began to emerge — beasts of shadow, with glowing eyes and sinewy forms that shifted like mist. They were not like any creatures the wolves had encountered before. Their movements were unnaturally fast, and their forms seemed to flicker, as if they were more than flesh and bone. These were the enemies of the wilds, the predators born of darkness itself, moving with an eerie fluidity that made them appear both real and unreal.

The wolves could hear their low, guttural growls, almost like whispers carried by the wind. The creatures were closing in, each step taken in the shadows bringing them closer to the pack. They moved with a malevolent intelligence, calculating and precise, understanding the pack's every move. The wolves had been tested by the forest before, but now they faced a threat that was as much psychological as physical. The creatures in the shadows were not just stalking the pack; they were trying to break their unity, to sow doubt and fear.

In that moment, the pack knew they had no choice but to fight. The forest had tested them with its twisted pines and shadows, but it was now time to face the true terror lurking in its depths. The wolves, united in their purpose and their bond, prepared to defend their territory, their pack, and their future. Whatever these foes were, the wolves would meet them with strength, courage, and the unyielding resolve to survive. The battle had begun.

Chapter 5
The Moonlit Ritual

The moon hung high in the sky, casting its silver light through the thick canopy of the forest. The pack had gathered, silent and expectant, beneath its glow. Tonight was a night like no other—an ancient ceremony that had been performed by their ancestors for countless generations. The air was thick with the scent of the earth, the hum of the forest around them blending with the quiet anticipation that filled the clearing. The ritual was not one to be taken lightly; it was a sacred tradition that bound the wolves not just to each other, but to the very essence of the land they protected. It was a ceremony of renewal, a reaffirmation of the pack's strength, and a powerful connection to the forces that governed their world.

The Alpha stood at the head of the gathering, their posture proud and commanding. Their eyes were fixed on the sky, the full moon reflecting in their gaze. Tonight, they would lead the pack through the ritual, but the ceremony was not just a matter of tradition. It was necessary to ensure that the pack remained strong, that their bond with the land and its ancient spirits remained unbroken. The wolves knew that in times of uncertainty, such ceremonies were vital. The ritual was a means of fortifying their unity and preparing them for the trials ahead. The bond of the pack was what kept them together, but it was the ritual that reminded them of the depth of that bond.

The pack moved as one, stepping carefully into position around the Alpha. The clearing was bathed in the soft light of the moon, casting long shadows on the forest floor. Each wolf took their place, their eyes fixed on the Alpha, awaiting the first sign that the ceremony had begun. There was no need for words. The ritual spoke through action, through the ancient gestures that had been passed down through the ages. As the Alpha raised their head to the sky, a single, powerful howl filled the air a call that resonated with the power of the land itself. The wolves joined in, their howls rising in harmony, a chorus of unity and strength.

Tonight, as the moonlight bathed them, the pack would perform the secret ceremony. It was a ritual that would bind them to the earth, to the spirits, and to each other in ways that were not always understood, but always felt. The blood of the pack would flow through the ritual, linking their past with their present, ensuring that they remained a force not just of survival, but of protection, loyalty, and strength. As the wolves stood beneath the watchful eyes of the moon, they knew that the ritual would prepare them for the challenges that lay ahead. They were not just wolves in the forest; they were its guardians, its protectors, and they were united in purpose and in spirit.

The Secret Ceremony

The Secret Ceremony was an ancient tradition that only the wolves truly understood, passed down through countless generations. It was not a ritual that could be observed by just anyone, and it was never performed in the light of day. The ceremony took place under the cover of darkness, when the moon was at its fullest, casting its pale light over the forest in a soft, silvery glow. The pack, united and solemn, gathered in a sacred clearing deep within the heart of the wilds an area where the trees grew taller and the earth felt alive with magic. The space was hidden from prying eyes, protected by the very forest itself. The ceremony was as much about the secrecy of its location as it was about the act itself. To witness the ritual was to step into the ancient heart of the wolves' existence, a place where time and the mortal world held no sway.

As the wolves assembled, the Alpha led them in silence. Their movements were measured, precise, as they approached the center of the clearing where the ritual would unfold. There was no need for words—each wolf knew their role in the ceremony. The air around them seemed to hum with anticipation, thick with the weight of history. The wind itself seemed to pause, holding its breath, as if even the natural world was aware that something significant was about to transpire.

The Alpha, standing at the center of the clearing, began the ceremony with a single, deliberate motion. Their eyes were fixed on the sky, their muzzle raised to the heavens as they silently communicated with the land. The wolves followed suit, taking their places in a wide circle around the Alpha. This was not a time for disruption or uncertainty; the ritual required complete focus, absolute devotion to the pack's unity, and an unwavering trust in the ancient forces that guided them.

As the Alpha began to chant, their voice low and reverberating, the sound carried through the trees. The chant was not in any language known to the wolves of the present. It was an ancient tongue, older than the pack itself, older than the land. The words were imbued with power, each syllable a binding force that connected the wolves to the spirits of their ancestors, to the earth, to the forces of nature that governed their lives. The chant was not simply a prayer—it was an invocation, a call to the spirits of the forest to witness the wolves' unity and to protect them in the trials to come.

The ritual required the wolves to offer their blood—a symbolic act that bound them together as a pack and reminded them of the sacrifice and loyalty that their bond demanded. The Alpha, standing as the leader and representative of the pack, took the first step. With a swift motion, they used their claws to draw a shallow cut along their own side, their blood dripping onto the earth. The pack followed, each wolf offering a small portion of their own life force, a drop of blood that fell onto the ground as a reminder of their shared purpose.

As the blood touched the earth, a subtle shift seemed to pass through the forest. The trees groaned in the wind, as though answering the call, their roots sinking deeper into the earth. The forest itself seemed to pulse, the land alive with the energy of the wolves' devotion. The bond between them, both physical and spiritual, grew stronger with every drop of blood, a connection that tied them to the land, to each other, and to the ancestors who had come before them.

The ceremony reached its climax as the wolves raised their heads to the sky, their howls rising in unison. It was not a call of aggression or challenge, but a song of unity, a song that resonated with the deepest parts of their souls. The wolves were not just packmates. They were family, bound by more than just blood they were bound by their connection to the earth, to the spirits, and to the ancient forces that had shaped their world.

As the final notes of the howl echoed through the night, the pack stood in silence, their heads bowed in reverence. The Secret Ceremony had been completed, and the wolves had reaffirmed their place in the world. They were ready to face whatever trials awaited them, united in their strength, in their loyalty, and in their shared purpose. The forest had witnessed their bond, and the spirits had heard their call. The wolves were no longer just survivors in the wild. They were its protectors, its children, and its champions.

Blood of the Pack

The Blood of the Pack was more than just a symbol of life. It was the foundation upon which their unity was built, a bond forged through generations of shared trials, sacrifices, and triumphs. The wolves understood this intimately, for their strength did not come from their individual power, but from the collective force of the pack. Blood, in the world of the wolves, was not just a physical substance. It was the very essence of who they were, the thread that tied them together and bound them to the land they protected.

As the pack gathered in the heart of the forest for the sacred ceremony, the air around them thickened with the gravity of what was about to unfold. The Blood of the Pack was a rite that required not just strength but sacrifice. The ritual was performed once every season, at the full moon, when the pack would gather to reaffirm their loyalty and commitment to each other and to their Alpha. It was a reminder that their survival depended not just on the power of the individual, but on the strength of the group. The Alpha stood at the center, their presence commanding, yet humbling, for they knew that their leadership was only as strong as the wolves they led.

The pack circled the Alpha, their bodies tense with anticipation. Each wolf, from the eldest to the youngest, knew their role in the ceremony. There were no words spoken, only the exchange of glances, the quiet, unspoken communication that existed between them. They were a family, and the Blood of the Pack was a promise they made to one another: to stand united, to fight together, and to protect one another at all costs.

The ritual began with the Alpha, who stood tall and proud, their eyes searching the faces of each member of the pack. The first step was a shared moment of silence, as the wolves acknowledged the importance of the ceremony. The Alpha then dipped their head, drawing a single drop of blood from their own side with a swift claw. The blood fell onto the earth beneath them, a symbol of their commitment to the land and to the pack. This blood was a powerful offering, a gift to the spirits that watched over them, ensuring their protection and guidance.

One by one, each wolf stepped forward. The pack's youngest members were the first to offer their blood, a small, yet significant sacrifice, symbolic of their devotion to the pack and their future in it. With a quick motion, they made a shallow cut along their skin, allowing their blood to drip onto the ground. As they did, the older members of the pack followed, their cuts deeper, their sacrifice greater. The blood of the pack stained the earth, mingling with the Alpha's own offering. The moment was sacred, for the pack's blood was not just their life force; it was the binding force that held them together.

As each wolf offered their blood, they felt a shift within themselves. The blood that touched the earth seemed to ignite the forest around them, filling the air with a quiet hum of energy. It was as if the very ground beneath their paws was alive, resonating with the power of their collective sacrifice. The wolves stood taller, their bond strengthened with each drop, their unity made unbreakable. The Alpha watched with quiet pride, knowing that this ritual, this offering, was what kept the pack strong.

The Blood of the Pack was not just about survival. It was about understanding the depth of their connection to one another, their shared history, and their shared future. In that moment, under the pale light of the moon, the wolves knew that they would face whatever challenges the world threw at them together. The pack was a family, and the blood they had offered to the earth was a promise that they would never falter, never break, no matter the trials ahead. They were bound by more than just blood—they were bound by their loyalty, their strength, and their unshakable bond.

Under the Watchful Eyes of the Moon

Under the Watchful Eyes of the Moon, the wolves gathered in the clearing, their forms silhouetted against the soft, silvery light that poured down from the heavens. The moon, full and radiant, hung high in the night sky, casting its ethereal glow across the land. It was a symbol of both power and mystery, a silent guardian of the wolves' existence. The forest, once filled with the natural rhythms of life, now seemed still, as if the very earth itself was holding its breath in reverence of the moon. In this sacred moment, everything felt heightened, charged with an ancient energy that bound the wolves to the world around them and to each other. This was not merely the light of a celestial body it was the presence of something older, something eternal, watching over them.

The pack stood still, their eyes lifted toward the moon. There was a quiet understanding among them, a recognition that they were not just wolves of the wild they were creatures of the earth and the sky, connected to forces beyond their comprehension. The moon was more than just a distant orb. It was a force of nature, an ancient power that held sway over the very cycles of life. It controlled the tides, the seasons, and the rhythms of the animals, and the wolves, more than any other creature, were deeply attuned to its pull. Under its watchful eyes, they could feel its power surge within them, stirring their instincts, sharpening their senses, and igniting the ancient connection they shared with the land.

As the Alpha stood at the head of the pack, their gaze never leaving the moon, they knew that the moment had arrived. The ritual they had begun was not merely a traditionit was a call to the spirits of the earth, a plea for strength, guidance, and protection. The wolves had always known the power of the moon, but tonight, its presence was felt more keenly than ever. The Alpha's howl, which had begun as a quiet murmur of acknowledgment, now grew louder, more resonant. It filled the air, echoing through the trees, reverberating against the hills and the distant mountains. It was a call to the forest itself, a summons to the ancient forces that governed their world.

One by one, the pack joined in, their howls rising in harmony. The sound of their voices, unified in purpose, carried far into the night, their song merging with the night wind. The wolves' collective howl was a symbol of their strength and unity, a pledge to protect the forest, to defend their pack, and to honor the land they called home. The moon, in all its quiet majesty, watched them, its light bathing them in its glow, as if to say that they were not alone that it, too, stood by them in their fight for survival.

But the Watchful Eyes of the Moon were not just a comforting presence. They were a reminder of the challenges that lay ahead. The moon, in all its power, had seen countless battles fought under its light wars of nature, of life and death, of struggle and sacrifice. It had witnessed the rise and fall of countless creatures, and it would bear witness to the wolves' trials as well. There would be challenges ahead, forces beyond their control, but as long as the moon watched over them, the wolves knew they would not face them alone.

Under the moon's gaze, the pack felt both humble and empowered. Their connection to the land, to each other, and to the forces that shaped their world was clear in this moment. The moon's light was not just a symbol of beauty it was a beacon of hope, strength, and guidance. In its glow, the wolves knew they were part of something larger, something eternal. Under the Watchful Eyes of the Moon, the pack stood united, ready to face whatever the wilds had in store for them, knowing that the forces of nature were aligned in their favor.

Chapter 6
The Pack's Strength

The pack's strength was not simply in their physical prowess, but in their unity. Each wolf, from the youngest to the oldest, contributed to the whole, and it was their shared bond that allowed them to overcome the challenges that came their way. In times of peace, it was easy to forget the depth of this connection, as the pack moved through the forest with ease, hunting, playing, and resting together. But in moments of adversity, when the world seemed to turn against them, their unity became their greatest weapon. It was in these moments that the wolves were reminded of what truly made them powerful—their unwavering loyalty to one another, their willingness to fight side by side, and their trust in their Alpha.

The Alpha, a figure of leadership and strength, had always known the power of the pack's unity. As the leader, they were the one who held the wolves together, guiding them through the darkest times and making the difficult decisions when the need arose. But the Alpha also understood that their strength alone was not enough to protect the pack. It was the collective will of the wolves that would see them through the trials ahead. The bond between them was something that no outside force could break, and it was this unbreakable connection that would allow them to face the coming challenges with courage and resolve.

The Alpha's command was not simply a call to action—it was a declaration of the pack's resolve, a reminder that they stood together, no matter the odds. The pack trusted their Alpha, not because of fear, but because of the deep respect they had for their leader's wisdom and strength. The Alpha's decisions were made with the pack's best interests in mind, and in turn, the pack followed them with unwavering loyalty. This bond, built on years of shared experiences and sacrifices, was the foundation of the pack's strength.

But the true power of the pack lay in the bond of blood and fur, a connection that ran deeper than anything physical. The wolves were not just a group of individuals; they were a family, bound by more than just loyalty—they were bound by a shared purpose and an understanding that their survival depended on one another. This bond transcended the battlefield, woven into every howl, every shared hunt, and every moment of rest. The strength of the pack was a strength that could not be measured by size or power alone; it was a strength born of love, sacrifice, and an unbreakable bond. Together, the wolves stood ready to face whatever the future had in store.

Unity in the face of adversity

Unity in the face of adversity was the very essence of the wolves' existence, a principle that had guided them through countless trials, tests, and hardships. It was not something that came easily; it was forged through struggle, tempered by time, and passed down through the generations as the core of their survival. The pack knew that when darkness closed in, when the world seemed stacked against them, their greatest strength was not in their individual power, but in their ability to stand together, united in purpose and in spirit.

The wolves were creatures of instinct, and yet, their unity was a conscious choice a bond built on trust, respect, and loyalty. Each wolf had their place within the pack, and each role was vital to their survival. From the youngest pup to the eldest wolf, every member contributed to the strength of the whole. The pack was an intricate network of interconnected lives, each individual supporting the others, and through this web of connection, they could weather any storm. It was the understanding that they were stronger together, that the survival of one was tied to the survival of all, that made them a force to be reckoned with.

When adversity struck, the pack did not falter. They faced challenges that could have broken them fierce predators from outside their territory, harsh winters that tested their endurance, and threats that came from within, challenging their unity and trust. But no matter the threat, they always came back to one another. The wolves knew that to survive, they could not afford to let fear or doubt fracture their bond. In the face of the unknown, when they felt the sting of vulnerability, it was their unity that pulled them through.

The Alpha, who stood as the symbol of the pack's leadership, knew the true weight of this unity. Their role was not to rule with fear or command by force, but to guide the pack with wisdom, to be the unwavering anchor in the storm. In moments of peril, when the pack was pushed to their limits, it was the Alpha's ability to inspire and unite that made the difference. They were the one who reminded the pack of their strength, of the bond they shared. They understood that the pack's power was in their unity, and when it was tested, they were there to hold them together.

In times of danger, when the pack was threatened, the unity of their howl became their weapon. The wolves would stand side by side, their eyes fierce with determination, their voices rising in unison. It was a cry that echoed through the forest, a reminder that no matter what came their way, they would face it together. The howl, which had always been a song of the wild, became a battle cry—a declaration of their resolve. The very air would vibrate with the power of their unity, an energy so strong that it could not be ignored.

The strength of the pack lay in the moments when they came together, their shared purpose burning bright even in the darkest of times. It was in these moments that their true power was revealed. When one wolf faltered, another was there to lift them up. When fear crept in, the pack would surround them, offering comfort and support, reminding each member that they were never alone. Their strength was not in their size or their speed, but in their unwavering commitment to each other.

In the face of adversity, the wolves knew that their survival depended on the unity they shared. It was a bond that could not be broken by hardship or fear, for it was forged in the fires of shared struggle. Together, they were unstoppable. Together, they were unbreakable.

The Alpha's Command

The Alpha's Command was more than just an order. It was a force that reverberated through the pack, a call to action that transcended mere words. The Alpha did not rule through force or fear, but through respect, wisdom, and the undeniable strength of their leadership. Their command was not just a spoken directive; it was an embodiment of the pack's collective will, a symbol of unity and resolve that the wolves could not ignore. When the Alpha spoke, it was as if the forest itself listened, and the very air seemed to still in anticipation of their next words.

The Alpha was not simply the strongest or the fastest; their power came from their ability to guide the pack through the storm, to keep the wolves united even in the face of overwhelming odds. Their command was not born of ego, but of necessity. The pack was built on cooperation, trust, and shared strength. Without a leader who could inspire and direct them, the pack would fall into disarray. The Alpha's role was to ensure that the pack remained focused, that their shared purpose and bond remained intact. When danger loomed, when the pack faced threats from within or without, the Alpha's command was what held them together, grounding them in their shared identity.

In moments of uncertainty, the Alpha's command would rise above the fear and confusion. It was a simple gesture, a single word or movement, but its effect was immediate. When the pack hesitated, unsure of what action to take, the Alpha would step forward, their presence alone enough to cut through the tension. Their voice, steady and firm, would pierce the silence, delivering their command with the weight of authority that could not be questioned. The wolves knew that to defy the Alpha was to defy the pack itself. The Alpha's decisions were made for the good of the whole, and the pack trusted in the wisdom behind them.

But the Alpha's command was not just about authority. It was about understanding the pack's needs, their strengths, and their weaknesses. The Alpha knew that leadership was not about controlling every action, but about knowing when to give direction and when to step back. There were moments when the Alpha's command was subtle, a quiet nudge in the right direction, allowing the wolves to find their own way. In other moments, the command was more direct, a rallying cry that brought the pack together in the face of danger. Whatever the situation, the Alpha's command was always rooted in the pack's well-being and survival.

The pack, for their part, followed the Alpha without question, not because they feared the consequences of disobedience, but because they respected their leader's ability to see the bigger picture. The Alpha did not lead with arrogance, but with humility and empathy. They understood the importance of each wolf within the pack, and their command was always issued with that understanding in mind. The Alpha was not just the leader; they were the protector, the guide, and the embodiment of the pack's spirit.

When the pack faced a threat, the Alpha's command was the spark that ignited their resolve. It was a call to arms, a declaration that the pack would not be defeated. The wolves, united by the Alpha's strength, would rise together, ready to face whatever dangers lay ahead. In those moments, the Alpha's command was more than just an order it was the embodiment of the pack's strength, their unity, and their unshakable belief in their survival. The Alpha's voice carried the weight of their entire world, and with it, the pack moved as one, unstoppable in their determination and loyalty.

Bond of Blood and Fur

The Bond of Blood and Fur was the unspoken force that held the pack together, a connection that ran deeper than mere physical proximity or shared territory. It was a bond forged through generations, shaped by the struggles of survival, the loyalty that came with shared hardship, and the unbreakable trust between the wolves. This bond was not something that could be easily seen or measured. It was woven into the fabric of their lives, part of their very being, and was the foundation of their strength. The pack was not just a group of individuals who happened to live together; it was a family, bound by blood, by shared experiences, and by the ties that connected their spirits as much as their bodies.

At the heart of this bond was the Alpha, whose bloodline held a special place in the pack's history. The Alpha was more than just a leader—they were a living embodiment of the pack's strength, spirit, and unity. The Alpha's blood was intertwined with the very land they protected, carrying with it the power of generations past. It was said that the first Alpha, the progenitor of their line, had been chosen by the land itself, and their blood had been passed down through the ages, carrying with it the wisdom and strength of their ancestors. When the Alpha spoke, the pack listened, not just because they held authority, but because their blood was the thread that connected the pack to its past, to its identity, and to the land that sustained them.

But the Bond of Blood and Fur was not only about the Alpha. It was about every member of the pack, from the youngest pup to the oldest wolf. The pack understood that they were all interdependent, each member contributing to the whole in unique ways. The bond they shared was not just a physical one, but an emotional and spiritual connection that defined them. When one wolf hurt, they all felt it. When one wolf succeeded, they all celebrated. They were a collective, a unit, and no individual was ever truly alone. Their fur, thick and intertwined, symbolized the strength that came from their unity. When they stood together, shoulder to shoulder, their strength was greater than the sum of their parts.

The blood of the pack was a reminder of their shared history, but the fur that coated their bodies symbolized the closeness of their connection. It was through their fur that they could communicate in ways that words could not express. The brush of a tail, the nudge of a nose, the shared warmth of a body curled close for sleep—these were the moments that deepened the bond between the wolves. They understood each other in ways that went beyond language. They could sense the slightest change in each other's mood, could feel the tension in the air before a fight or the joy before a hunt. The pack's fur was a visible sign of their unity, their closeness, and their trust in one another.

This bond was most evident in moments of adversity. When the pack faced a challenge, whether it was a fierce predator encroaching on their territory or the harshness of a winter storm, the Bond of Blood and Fur became their greatest strength. In those moments, when everything else seemed uncertain, they could count on each other. The bond they shared made them resilient, able to withstand trials that would break lesser creatures. It was in the fiercest moments of battle or the quietest moments of rest that the bond was most apparent. When one wolf fell, the others would rise to lift them, to protect them, and to ensure that they never stood alone.

Through the Bond of Blood and Fur, the pack was not just a group of wolves. It was a family, a collective spirit that transcended individual needs and desires. This bond ensured that the wolves would survive, not just through strength, but through their unwavering connection to one another. It was this bond that made the pack unstoppable. When they stood together, their blood and fur intertwined, they were more than just wolves—they were a force of nature, invincible and eternal.

Chapter 7
The Shattered Peace

The forest, which had once been a sanctuary of peace and unity, now trembled under the weight of change. The calm that had defined the wolves' existence for so long had begun to crack, and with it, the fragile harmony that had bound the pack together. The Shattered Peace marked the beginning of a tumultuous period, a time when the wolves would be tested not just by external forces, but by the cracks that were beginning to form within their own ranks. The tranquility of the forest, once uninterrupted, was now threatened by the presence of intruders at the gates—forces from beyond their borders that sought to disrupt the balance of the land.

As the pack gathered in the heart of the forest, the unease was palpable. The intruders, who had appeared without warning, were unlike anything the pack had encountered before. They were a reminder that the wilderness was never as safe as it seemed, that the land could be encroached upon by forces that sought to claim it for their own. Their arrival set off a chain of events that would unravel not only the pack's external peace but also the delicate relationships between the wolves and their allies. What had once been a unified front began to fracture, as tensions among allies grew, and loyalties were questioned. The pack's strength had always relied on its unity, but now, with these intruders stirring discord, that unity was being tested in ways that no one had anticipated.

As the pack grappled with the threat posed by the intruders, deeper divisions began to emerge. The wolves, who had once fought side by side, began to argue over how to handle the situation. Some felt that the pack should stand firm, defending their territory with everything they had. Others, more cautious, argued for a more diplomatic approach, seeking to negotiate with the intruders and avoid unnecessary bloodshed. The Alpha, who had always been a steady force, now found themselves caught between the two factions, struggling to maintain control over the pack while navigating the rising tensions among their own wolves.

The fracture was not just within the pack; it extended to their allies as well. The alliances that had been forged over the years, based on mutual respect and shared goals, began to crumble as old wounds resurfaced and mistrust took root. What had once been a collective force, bound by the same purpose, was now splintering. The wolves were faced with a hard truth: their unity was no longer guaranteed, and the very foundation of their strength was under threat. The pack's once unshakable bond was now fragile, and in the face of these external and internal challenges, they had to decide whether they would fall apart or rise stronger than before. The peace they had once known was shattered, and now the true test of their strength was about to begin.

Intruders at the Gates

The scent of the intruders was the first sign, faint but unmistakable, drifting on the wind like an unwanted guest. At first, the pack took no notice of it, dismissing it as the usual fluctuations of the forest. But soon, as the scent grew stronger, a sense of unease settled over the wolves. There was something different about this intrusion, something that set the hairs on the back of their necks on edge. The Alpha, ever vigilant, was the first to acknowledge the danger. The familiar boundaries of their territory had been breached, and something dark and foreign had entered their world.

The Alpha stood at the edge of the pack's territory, eyes scanning the horizon with a quiet intensity. The wind carried the scent again, this time more pronounced, and it was clear—these were not creatures of the forest. They were outsiders, intruders with no respect for the land that the wolves had fought so hard to protect. Their presence was like a poison, slowly seeping into the forest and poisoning the very air they breathed. The pack's territory was sacred, a place they had fought to defend for generations, and the wolves knew that to let such trespassers remain was a threat to everything they had built.

The first sign of the intruders' physical presence came a few days later, when strange tracks were found near the boundary of their land. The tracks were large, heavy, and unmistakable in their irregularity. They did not belong to any animal the wolves knew. These intruders had come in force, leaving behind deep, wide prints in the soft earth. It was clear that they were not here by accident. The wolves immediately recognized that the intruders had come for something. Whether it was the wolves' territory, their resources, or something even more ominous, it was impossible to tell. But the fact that they had dared to come this far was a direct challenge to the pack's way of life.

The Alpha called the pack together. The air around them was thick with tension, the wolves' eyes flashing with a mix of uncertainty and anger. It was clear that the time for caution had passed. The pack would have to confront this threat head-on. There was no way to avoid the confrontation. The intruders had crossed into their land, and now they had to be dealt with, one way or another.

The pack moved swiftly, navigating the forest with practiced stealth, the wolves' movements synchronized as they ventured toward the outer edges of their territory. The intruders were not far behind. They had made no attempt to hide their presence; their steps were deliberate and loud, marking their encroachment on the wolves' home. As the pack neared the border, they spotted the intruders—three figures, large and imposing, moving with a confidence that was both unsettling and dangerous. They were unlike any predators the wolves had faced before. They walked on two legs, tall and muscular, with strange, elongated features and eyes that glowed unnaturally in the moonlight.

The Alpha, ever the leader, approached the intruders cautiously, signaling to the pack to stay back and observe. They could feel the weight of the situation pressing down on them. These were not mere trespassers; they were a force to be reckoned with. The intruders had come with purpose, and their presence posed a threat the pack could not ignore. As the Alpha stepped forward, the intruders paused, their eyes locking with the Alpha's in a silent, yet charged moment of tension. For a long moment, no one moved. It was a standoff, an unspoken challenge hanging between them.

Then, without warning, one of the intruders spoke in a low, gravelly voice. "We seek what is ours," they said, their words filled with a strange authority. The pack bristled at the tone, but the Alpha remained calm, steady. "This is our land," the Alpha replied, their voice unwavering. "You are not welcome here." The tension between them grew thicker, as if the forest itself was holding its breath, waiting for what would come next.

The intruders made no immediate move to retreat. Instead, they stood their ground, their eyes scanning the pack, sizing them up. It was clear that they had no intention of leaving quietly. A fight was inevitable, but the Alpha knew they could not afford to be rash. The pack had always fought for survival, but they had never faced an enemy like this. The intruders were different—stronger, more cunning, and far more dangerous than anything the wolves had encountered in the past.

The Alpha gave a sharp, low growl, signaling for the pack to retreat. The wolves backed away, eyes never leaving the intruders. The Alpha understood that a direct confrontation now would lead to unnecessary bloodshed. They needed to understand the intruders' intentions, to learn more about who or what they were. The wolves' territory was sacred, and they would not allow it to be taken without a fight, but they could not afford to make a misstep. The intruders at the gates were a warning—one that the wolves could not ignore. The battle for their land, for their future, had only just begun.

Tensions Among Allies

Tensions Among Allies began to rise the moment the pack found themselves face-to-face with the intruders. At first, the wolves were united in their shared purpose—to defend their land, protect the Alpha, and secure their future. But as the presence of the trespassers grew more insistent, something else began to stir among the wolves. What was meant to be a unified front slowly shifted into a divided one. The unity that had always been their greatest strength began to crack, revealing vulnerabilities that had long been buried.

It was subtle at first, a quiet murmur in the back of the pack's mind, a flicker of uncertainty that slowly spread through their ranks. The initial shock of the intruders' arrival had given way to confusion, and as the wolves assessed their options, the cracks started to show. The younger wolves, more eager and quick to action, wanted to strike immediately. They were strong, full of energy, and hungry for a fight. They had never known anything but unity in the pack and the hunt, and now, standing at the precipice of an unknown challenge, they were ready to defend their land, no matter the cost. To them, the intruders were a threat that needed to be eliminated as soon as possible, without hesitation.

But the older wolves, the seasoned warriors who had seen many seasons of peace and turmoil alike, were more cautious. They had lived through countless battles, and their wisdom came from experience. They knew that the wolves' greatest strength lay not just in their physical might, but in their ability to think, to outsmart their enemies, and to make decisions with the survival of the pack in mind. A rash move could have disastrous consequences, and the cost of a direct confrontation could be too high. The older wolves spoke of patience, of waiting for the right moment to strike, and they urged the pack to consider their options carefully.

At first, the differences in opinion were merely a matter of perspective. The younger wolves, eager to prove themselves, challenged the older ones. The older wolves, in turn, called for caution and restraint. Tensions simmered, but the pack maintained its composure, listening to both sides. The Alpha, as always, tried to maintain balance, knowing that leadership required both strength and wisdom. But even the Alpha, the steady pillar of the pack, could feel the pressure mounting. They knew that the decision would need to be made soon, and that the pack's unity was on the line.

As the days passed and the threat of the intruders loomed ever closer, the division within the pack grew sharper. The younger wolves began to question the older wolves' reluctance to act. They accused them of being too slow, too cautious, and too afraid to defend what was theirs. These voices, once filled with respect for the wisdom of the elders, now carried an edge of frustration. They argued that the pack's future was at risk, and that waiting was the same as surrendering. The very thing that had always made the pack formidable—their unity—was starting to unravel, and it was being driven by the rising tension between those who wanted to strike and those who wanted to wait.

The older wolves, in turn, grew frustrated with the younger ones' eagerness. They had seen too much to be blinded by the adrenaline of youth. Their experience told them that there was more at stake than just the immediate threat. A hasty attack could easily provoke a war with the intruders, and the consequences of such a conflict were far-reaching. The stakes were not just about territory or survival; they were about the future of the pack, about the legacy they would leave behind. The older wolves began to question whether the younger wolves truly understood the weight of the decision they were so eager to make.

One night, under the pale light of the moon, the Alpha called the pack together. The tension between the factions had reached its breaking point. The wolves gathered in the clearing, their eyes filled with uncertainty and anger. The atmosphere was thick with unspoken words, and the Alpha could sense the fracture within their ranks. It was a painful moment, one that they knew would be difficult to heal, but it was necessary. The unity of the pack was slipping away, and if something wasn't done, it would be lost for good.

The Alpha stood before them, their presence commanding attention, their gaze steady and resolute. They spoke of the pack's history, of the countless battles they had faced together, and the many sacrifices that had been made to ensure their survival. They reminded the pack of the bond that had held them together through the darkest of times, of the strength that came from their unity. But most importantly, they spoke of trust—the trust that each wolf had in the other, the trust that had allowed them to survive when others had failed.

The Alpha made it clear that the decision to face the intruders could not be taken lightly. It was not a question of strength, but of strategy, of ensuring that the pack's future was not sacrificed in the heat of the moment. The wolves could fight and die, or they could fight and survive. The choice was theirs, but it had to be made together. The Alpha called for the younger wolves to trust in the wisdom of the elders, and for the older wolves to respect the urgency felt by the younger members. Only through compromise, only through truly listening to each other, could the pack move forward.

For a long while, there was silence. The wolves, divided by their emotions, seemed unwilling to budge. But slowly, the younger wolves began to listen, their fiery spirits dampened by the gravity of the situation. The older wolves, in turn, acknowledged the urgency of the younger wolves' concerns. It wasn't about one side winning or the other losing—it was about the pack as a whole.

At last, the Alpha spoke again, their voice calm and commanding. "We are stronger together," they said, their words carrying the weight of generations of wisdom. "We will fight as one, united, and we will face whatever comes with the strength of our bond. But we will not rush blindly into the storm. We will plan, and we will strike when the time is right."

And with that, the pack, fractured though they were, began to come together once more. The tension was not gone, but it had been channeled into a shared purpose. The pack was divided no longer by their differences, but united by the singular understanding that only through unity could they overcome the challenges ahead. Together, they would face the intruders—not as factions, but as one.

The Fractured Alliance

The Fractured Alliance was a deep wound that, for the first time in many seasons, threatened to tear apart the very fabric of the wolves' survival. What had once been a tight-knit group, bound by loyalty, trust, and shared purpose, now stood divided. The pack's strength had always rested on their unity, a unity that had been forged through years of collective hardship and triumph. But now, with the arrival of the intruders, the bond between the wolves began to unravel. Tensions, which had long been bubbling beneath the surface, finally broke through, exposing the cracks in their relationships.

At the heart of the fracture was the differing approach to the intruders' encroachment. The younger wolves, full of energy and fervor, were ready for immediate action. They saw the intrusion as an attack on their land, their home, and their heritage. For them, there was no time for hesitation or diplomacy; their only focus was to defend their territory and take back what was rightfully theirs. Their confidence was fueled by the belief that they were strong enough to face any threat head-on, no matter the cost. In their eyes, the longer they waited, the more vulnerable they became. The intruders could not be allowed to establish themselves on their land. To them, the Alpha's cautious approach seemed like hesitation, a sign of weakness. This growing frustration was voiced more and more openly, leading to conflict within the pack.

The older wolves, however, saw the situation through a more experienced lens. They had lived through countless struggles, some of which had been won with force, others with patience. They understood that the pack's survival depended not just on brute strength, but on intelligence, strategy, and foresight. The pack had long since learned the value of playing the long game—sometimes it was necessary to hold back, to observe, and to wait for the right moment to strike. The older wolves feared that rushing into battle would lead to unnecessary losses, a thought that deeply disturbed them. They had no illusions about the cost of war, and they knew that the wolves could not afford to risk everything on a rash decision. Their position was clear: they believed in a cautious approach, one that involved careful planning, negotiation if possible, and, above all, patience.

As the divide between the younger and older wolves deepened, the pack's unity began to erode. The younger wolves, feeling that their voices were being ignored, began to challenge the older wolves openly. Disputes broke out during meetings, with accusations thrown from both sides. "We cannot afford to wait!" the younger wolves would argue. "Every moment we hesitate, they grow stronger." In response, the older wolves would retort, "We are not weak for waiting. We are wise. You are blinded by your impatience." The tension was palpable, and with every argument, the pack's bond weakened.

The Alpha, usually a steady presence at the center of the pack, found themselves caught in the middle of this growing rift. They understood the fears of both sides. They had long trusted in the wisdom of the elders and the fiery spirit of the young. The challenge now was to unite the pack before the fracture became permanent. The Alpha knew that the wolves could not survive if they were divided. In their minds, it wasn't just about defending the land—it was about defending the very thing that made them wolves: their unity. If they fell apart now, if the fracture became a permanent divide, the pack would be no more than a collection of individuals, and no matter how strong an individual wolf was, alone, they were nothing.

The Alpha called for a council meeting, a gathering that had not been held in many moons. This was not an ordinary meeting; it was a last attempt to salvage the pack's unity. The clearing where the wolves convened was tense with anticipation. The air was heavy with the weight of their differences. Wolves of all ages stood in a wide circle, their eyes filled with concern and uncertainty. The young wolves, though eager for action, kept their postures stiff, a silent protest against what they saw as unnecessary delay. The older wolves, though more composed, were no less anxious, their expressions drawn as they weighed the gravity of the situation. The Alpha stood at the center, their gaze sweeping over the gathered wolves, sensing the rift that now divided them.

"This is not just about the land," the Alpha began, their voice carrying across the clearing, calm yet firm. "This is about our future, our survival, and the legacy of the pack. We cannot afford to let our differences destroy us. What we have built together—the strength we draw from each other—is what makes us more than mere animals. It is what makes us a family."

The Alpha's words hung in the air, the weight of their truth settling over the pack. Yet, the divisions were not easily healed. "The land is ours by right!" a young wolf interjected, their voice filled with anger and frustration. "We cannot allow these intruders to stay. Our blood, our fur—our strength—are what defend it. The pack's legacy depends on it!" There was a ripple of agreement from the younger wolves, their hackles raised in defiance.

The Alpha turned their gaze to the older wolves. "And you, what do you suggest?" The question was not one of accusation, but of seeking understanding. "Should we wait until we are overrun? Should we risk the pack's future because we fear the cost of battle?"

The older wolves, wise from experience, knew that the path forward was not simple. "We have faced many challenges," one of the elders spoke, their voice quiet but strong. "And we have learned that strength alone does not ensure survival. We must not let fear guide our decisions. We must be clever in how we move forward. A battle fought recklessly is a battle lost."

The discussion raged on for hours, each side voicing their concerns, their frustrations, and their fears. But slowly, through the heat of the arguments and the pressure of the situation, something began to change. The wolves, despite their differences, began to realize that they all wanted the same thing: survival, unity, and the future of the pack. The younger wolves, though eager to fight, began to understand that rushing into battle might only ensure their defeat. The older wolves, though cautious, began to see the passion and determination of the younger wolves and understood that sometimes, action was necessary.

Finally, after hours of debate, the Alpha stepped forward, their voice cutting through the tension. "We will stand together," they said. "Not as factions, but as a unified pack. We will find a way to confront the intruders, but we will do it on our terms, when the time is right. We will use our strength, our wisdom, and our unity. If we act together, there is no force that can break us."

And in that moment, the pack understood. The fracture had not been healed completely, but it had been bridged. They would face the intruders, not divided, but united in their resolve. The Fractured Alliance had begun to mend, and the wolves knew that, together, they would stand against whatever challenges lay ahead.

Chapter 8
Blood and Betrayal

Blood and Betrayal would mark the darkest chapter in the pack's history, a turning point that shattered the trust and unity they had fought so hard to maintain. The pack had always prided itself on its loyalty—each member bound by the same purpose, fighting for the survival of the whole. But as with all great forces, the threat of treachery lingered in the shadows, waiting for the right moment to reveal itself. What began as a quiet undercurrent of doubt quickly spiraled into a full-blown betrayal, leaving the pack fractured and vulnerable.

It started with a friend—someone who had stood beside the Alpha and shared in the pack's trials. The betrayal was not born of malice at first; it was a subtle shift, a quiet erosion of trust. At first, the pack didn't see the signs, too focused on the external threats that loomed over them. But as the days wore on, the cracks began to show. A friend, once considered loyal, began to act in ways that were incongruent with the values they had once upheld. Whispers and rumors began to circulate, and soon, it became clear: the very wolf who had shared the Alpha's confidence was now working against them, conspiring with forces from the outside.

The realization that someone so close to them had turned was like a wound in the pack's heart. The knife in the back wasn't just a physical act—it was an emotional one. It was a betrayal that cut deep, not only because of the personal connection, but because it symbolized everything they feared. The pack had always feared the day when someone would put personal ambition above the good of the group, and now that day had come.

The aftermath of the treachery left the pack in turmoil. Trust, the very foundation of their strength, was now fractured. The Alpha, once unwavering in their leadership, found themselves questioning every decision, every gesture, and every word that had been spoken in the past. Was the betrayal inevitable, or was it a sign of something deeper—something they had missed? In the wake of the betrayal, the pack had to rebuild not just their territory, but their sense of trust. Could they move forward as a united force, or would this wound fester, tearing them apart from the inside? Blood and Betrayal would test them like never before, forcing them to confront the reality that the greatest dangers are not always the ones from outside—they are sometimes the ones closest to home.

A Friend Turned Foe

A Friend Turned Foe was the deepest betrayal the pack had ever known, a twist of fate that shattered their very foundation. It wasn't the first time the pack had faced external threats, nor would it be the last. The wilds were full of dangers—other predators, harsh winters, disease, and the ever-present encroachment of civilization. But these were threats the wolves could prepare for. They knew how to fight against these challenges. They knew how to protect each other. The pack had always prided itself on its unity, the unspoken bond that existed between each wolf. The strength of the pack was in their loyalty to one another, their shared history, and their unwavering commitment to the survival of the group. This unity, forged over years of shared hardship, was the pack's greatest asset, and it was something they thought could never be broken.

But this time, the danger came not from the wilderness, but from within. It started with a shift in behavior, something subtle at first, barely noticeable. A wolf who had once stood alongside the Alpha, who had fought by their side in countless battles, who had shared in the joys and burdens of leadership, began to act differently. The pack first noticed it in the quiet moments—the way the wolf would linger on the outskirts of group conversations, their eyes distant, their posture tense. It was easy to dismiss at first. The pack had other worries: the impending arrival of the intruders, the need to scout new hunting grounds, and the challenges of surviving through the harsh winter months. There was little time to focus on subtle changes in behavior, but in retrospect, those changes would prove to be the first signs of the treachery to come.

As time passed, the wolf's behavior grew more erratic. They began to question the Alpha's decisions, subtly at first, then more openly. They would challenge the Alpha's orders during council meetings, arguing for alternate strategies that seemed at odds with the pack's unity. It wasn't that the pack had never disagreed with their leader before—debate and discussion were common. But this felt different. The arguments were more forceful, more personal, and more frequent. The Alpha, ever the steady leader, dismissed these concerns as momentary lapses in judgment. The pack's strength was in its unity, and they believed that any disagreement could be resolved through calm discussion. But even the Alpha, who had always been a pillar of strength, began to feel the weight of the wolf's growing resistance.

The moment of truth came on a cold night, under the pale light of a waning moon. The wolves had just finished a hunt, and the pack was gathered near their den, sharing the spoils of their labor. The pack, as always, moved in unison, a seamless dance of coordination and trust. But that night, the atmosphere was different. The wolf who had once been a friend, a trusted ally, stood apart from the group. Their eyes were fixed on the Alpha, their expression unreadable. The tension was palpable.

The Alpha, sensing the unease in the air, called for a private word with the wolf. They stepped away from the group, into the shadows of the trees, where the wind was sharp and biting. The Alpha's voice was calm, steady, but there was a note of concern that hadn't been there before. "What is troubling you?" they asked, their gaze searching the wolf's face for the truth that had remained hidden for so long.

The wolf's response was not what the Alpha had expected. "I can no longer follow you," they said, their voice low and filled with something that the Alpha could not place—anger, regret, or perhaps both. "Your leadership has led us into stagnation. You are too focused on the old ways, too cautious. The world is changing, and you are too blind to see it."

The Alpha's heart sank. The words, though soft, struck like a blow. This wasn't a disagreement over tactics. This was an abandonment of everything the pack stood for. The trust they had shared, the unspoken bond that had kept them united through thick and thin, was being shattered in this moment. "What are you saying?" the Alpha asked, their voice barely above a whisper, as if they couldn't quite believe the reality of the situation.

"I'm saying that you've failed us," the wolf replied, stepping back, their eyes hardening. "You've failed the pack. The future is in power, not in unity. I've found another way. I've found others who see things as I do."

It was then that the full weight of the betrayal hit. The wolf wasn't simply disagreeing with the Alpha. They were aligning themselves with the intruders, with the very threat the pack had been preparing to face. The wolf had been working with the enemy from the inside, feeding them information, undermining the Alpha's leadership, and weakening the pack's resolve. The pack had been led to believe that the enemy at the gates was an external force, but the true danger had always been there, within their own ranks.

The Alpha stood frozen, their mind racing, trying to process the magnitude of the betrayal. The wolf, once a trusted friend, had become their greatest foe. In that moment, the weight of leadership felt unbearable. The Alpha had always known that the greatest threats came from the outside, from the harshness of the wild and the dangers of the hunt. But this was different. This was personal. This was a wound from within, a betrayal of the deepest kind.

The wolf, seeing the Alpha's hesitation, gave a final, bitter laugh. "You were never fit to lead. Your weakness will be our undoing." With that, they turned and disappeared into the night, their form swallowed by the darkness. The Alpha stood alone in the cold, the air thick with the scent of betrayal.

The pack would soon learn the truth, but it would be too late. The friend they had trusted, the wolf they had considered a part of their family, had become the very thing they feared: an enemy. The fractures within the pack would deepen, and the unity they had worked so hard to build would crumble in the wake of this betrayal. The Alpha, once certain in their role, now had to face a reality they had never prepared for—the one truth they had always feared: that sometimes, the greatest threat to survival came from the ones closest to you.

The Knife in the Back

The Knife in the Back was the moment the pack was irreparably changed. It wasn't just the physical act of betrayal that shattered them—it was the realization that they had been deceived by someone they had once called family. The wolf who had turned against them, once a trusted ally and friend, had gone beyond mere disagreement. They had actively undermined the pack from within, slowly and methodically, planting seeds of doubt and division. The betrayal was deep, a wound that cut to the heart of the wolves' unity, leaving them broken and unsure of whom they could trust.

It all began on that fateful night when the pack was gathered in the safety of their den, their usual camaraderie replaced by an unsettling silence. The tension in the air was thick with the weight of what had been left unsaid, the eyes of the younger wolves lingering nervously on the older members, who, for the first time, seemed unsure of their next move. The Alpha had been preoccupied with the approaching threat—the intruders at the gates—and had trusted that the pack would remain united in the face of danger. But something was off. The usual sense of solidarity was missing. The trust, which had always been the pack's greatest strength, felt fragile.

As the Alpha sat at the heart of the group, their mind was racing, trying to piece together what had happened. The pack had always faced challenges, always fought to defend their territory, but this felt different. This wasn't an external enemy—this was something far more insidious. The Alpha's gaze swept over the pack, noticing the subtle shift in the dynamics. The once reliable wolf, the one who had stood by their side in countless battles, now avoided eye contact, their posture tense, their movements erratic. The Alpha's instincts told them something was wrong, but they could not yet place the cause. It wasn't until the betrayal was revealed that everything fell into place.

It started as a whisper in the wind, a suspicion that slowly crept into the Alpha's thoughts, gnawing at them with increasing urgency. That night, as the pack slept, the Alpha followed their instincts. Stepping silently through the dense forest, they kept their distance from the others, moving cautiously in the shadows. The pack had always been a united front, but now the Alpha felt the weight of every step, as though they were walking on unstable ground.And then they saw it.

The once-trusted wolf, the one who had served as the Alpha's right paw, was not alone. They stood in the clearing, speaking in low tones to figures cloaked in shadow—figures that had no business being this close to their territory. The Alpha's heart sank. The figures were none other than the intruders, the very beings who had been circling their land, testing the pack's defenses. The wolf that had once been their ally was now standing beside the enemy, whispering secrets into their ears.

The Alpha felt the sting of betrayal wash over them like a cold wave. It wasn't just the actions of the wolf—it was the knowledge that they had been deceived, that the trust they had placed in them had been shattered in the darkest possible way. The wolf wasn't merely in alliance with the intruders—they were orchestrating the pack's downfall from within. The Alpha watched in disbelief as the wolf handed over crucial information—routes, weaknesses, even strategic plans for future hunts. The Alpha's breath caught in their throat. The pack was no longer safe.

In that moment, the knife in the back had already been thrust into the Alpha's heart. The betrayal had been set in motion long before the Alpha had even begun to suspect it. The wolf had taken advantage of their trust, using their proximity to the leader to gain access to sensitive information, and now, with the enemies so close to their borders, it was clear that the consequences would be dire. The pack, unknowingly led by the traitor, was walking into a trap.

The Alpha knew they could not let the pack find out just yet. If the truth came to light too soon, it would destroy them. The pack was already on the edge—distrust was spreading like wildfire. If word got out about the traitor, the division within the ranks would be impossible to contain. The Alpha had to act swiftly, quietly.

The next few days were filled with tension. The Alpha kept a close eye on the wolf who had betrayed them, but it was impossible to directly confront them without causing suspicion. Every moment felt like a ticking clock, the weight of the betrayal pressing down on the Alpha's shoulders. They could not allow the pack to fall apart, not now, not with the intruders so close. But the trust had been broken. It was only a matter of time before the pack would find out the truth.

The Alpha could feel the fracture deepening. The wolves, sensing the unease, began to turn on one another. The younger wolves, fueled by their impatience and desire for action, began to question the Alpha's leadership more openly, demanding answers that the Alpha was not ready to give. They felt the shift in the air—something was off, something was wrong within their own ranks, and they wanted answers. The Alpha knew they could not wait much longer. The time for secrecy was over. The pack had to know the truth, but how could they possibly explain that the very wolf they had trusted, the one who had stood at their side, had turned against them?

Finally, the Alpha made the decision to confront the traitor directly. Under the cover of night, away from the rest of the pack, the Alpha met with the wolf in a secluded part of the forest. The air between them was charged with anger and betrayal. The Alpha's voice was low but firm, filled with an edge of hurt that they could not hide.

"I trusted you," the Alpha said, their voice tight with emotion. "We fought together. You were supposed to be one of us."

The traitor's expression remained cold, almost detached. "Trust is a luxury we can no longer afford," they replied, their voice devoid of remorse. "I did what needed to be done. The pack was weak. You were weak."

The words cut deep, but the Alpha stood tall. "You sold us out. You sold me out."

The wolf stepped forward, their eyes flickering with a mix of disdain and calculation. "The pack needs to evolve. You've been holding them back. The new world is coming, and the strong will take what's theirs. I'm no longer bound by the old ways, and neither should you be."

The final blow came when the traitor revealed their true allegiance. They were not just acting for their own benefit; they had been promised power by the intruders in exchange for their loyalty. They had been working to weaken the pack from within, knowing that once the Alpha was deposed, the pack would be vulnerable and ripe for takeover.

In that moment, the Alpha knew what had to be done. The traitor had to be removed, for the sake of the pack, for the sake of survival. But the damage had already been done. The knife in the back had already been thrust, and the blood of the pack had been spilled—not just on the ground, but in their hearts. The trust was shattered, and the wolves could never return to the unity they had once known. The pack's future was now uncertain, torn apart by the treachery of someone they had once called family.

The Aftermath of Treachery

The aftermath of treachery was a deep wound, one that would not heal easily. It was a fracture in the very soul of the pack, a betrayal that could not be undone, no matter how much time passed or how hard they tried to forget. The consequences of the wolf's disloyalty echoed far beyond the simple act of betrayal. It rippled through the pack, weakening their resolve and testing their unity in ways they had never imagined. The Alpha, ever the steadfast leader, felt the weight of this betrayal more keenly than any wolf in the pack. It wasn't just the loss of a trusted ally—it was the realization that even the strongest bonds could be broken, that loyalty could be betrayed by the very wolves they had fought beside.

In the days following the discovery of the traitor's actions, the pack was on edge. Tensions that had already been simmering beneath the surface now boiled over. The younger wolves, who had once been eager to defend their territory and uphold the pack's strength, now found themselves questioning everything they had been taught. Could they trust each other? Could they trust the Alpha? The betrayal was not just a personal wound—it was a question of the very foundation of their survival. The pack had always relied on their unity to face the dangers of the wild, but now that unity had been shattered. How could they stand together when they no longer knew who could be trusted?

The older wolves, too, were shaken. They had seen their fair share of conflict, of bloodshed, but the treachery of one of their own struck at something deeper than mere strategy or battle tactics. It was an emotional blow, one that left them questioning their judgment. They had trusted the traitor, had fought alongside them, and now they wondered if they had missed the signs. Had they been too trusting? Were they blind to the growing divide within their ranks? The older wolves, who had always been the steadying force in the pack, now found themselves lost in their own doubts.

The Alpha, though steadfast, was no exception to the emotional toll. The weight of the betrayal was crushing, and it was not just the loss of the traitor but the realization of the vulnerability it exposed. The Alpha had always been the pillar of strength for the pack, but in the wake of this betrayal, they were forced to confront the fragility of their leadership. How could they lead a pack that was no longer whole? How could they restore trust, when that trust had been violated so deeply? Every decision, every command they gave, was now questioned, not just by the pack, but by themselves. They were the leader, the one who had sworn to protect the pack, but had they failed in this moment? Had they failed to see the signs, to keep their wolves safe from the very ones who had once been closest to them?

In the days that followed, the pack grew restless. The wolves could feel the change in the air. The once-solid unity between them had been replaced by an invisible barrier, a chasm that no amount of time could easily bridge. They had been betrayed by one of their own, and that betrayal stung deeper than any wound inflicted by an external enemy. The younger wolves began to question the older wolves, wondering if they had been too naïve, too trusting. The older wolves, in turn, began to wonder if they had been too protective, too slow to act, and now, they feared the damage that had been done.

The bond of blood and fur, which had always been the pack's greatest strength, seemed fragile now. The pack was no longer a unit that moved together as one. It was divided, torn between those who still held to the old ways and those who were questioning everything. The Alpha knew that they needed to restore the pack's unity, but the task ahead was monumental. They could no longer take for granted that the wolves would follow them without question. They needed to rebuild not just trust, but the very sense of belonging that had always been the heart of their pack.

The process of healing, of repairing the broken trust, began slowly and painfully. The Alpha called for a gathering, but it was different this time. There were no howls of celebration, no joyous reunions. The wolves gathered in silence, a somber reminder of how far they had fallen. The Alpha stood at the center, their eyes sweeping over the pack, knowing that their leadership had been challenged in ways they had never anticipated. The Alpha spoke, but their words were not as sure as they had once been. They spoke of unity, of the need for the pack to stand together, but the words felt hollow. Could the wolves believe in them again? Could the

Alpha lead them with the same conviction, knowing the seed of doubt had been sown?

The traitor's departure, though inevitable, left its mark. The Alpha's decision to banish the wolf who had betrayed them was not made lightly. It wasn't just a matter of exile—it was a painful acknowledgment that the pack had been irreparably changed. The traitor's departure was not a clean break; it left scars, not just in the land they had once shared, but in the wolves' hearts. For some, the banishment was a necessary act of justice; for others, it felt like a failure, a reminder that the pack had been divided. There was no victory in the aftermath, no sense of triumph in their survival. There was only a quiet, painful understanding that the price of betrayal was steep, and the cost of healing would be even greater.

In the days that followed, the pack moved with caution. They no longer spoke with the same sense of shared purpose. They hunted together, but there was an awkwardness in their movements, a hesitation in their actions. The wolves were no longer a united force, and the wilderness, once a place of security and safety, now felt vast and uncertain. The pack had faced external dangers, but this was different. The damage had come from within, and it was far harder to heal. The wolves, once united in their loyalty, now carried the weight of the betrayal in their hearts.

As the Alpha watched the pack move through the wilderness, they knew that the road to recovery would be long. There was no quick fix, no easy solution. The pack had been wounded, and the scars would remain, a reminder of the price they had paid for their misplaced trust. The only path forward was through time, through the slow rebuilding of what had been broken. The pack's strength, the very thing that had always defined them, would have to be earned again, piece by piece, trust by trust. The Aftermath of Treachery had marked the wolves, but it was not the end. It was the beginning of their fight for survival, not against an enemy at their gates, but against the invisible wounds that now threatened to tear them apart from the inside.

Chapter 9
The Dark Hunter

The arrival of The Dark Hunter marked a new and terrifying chapter in the pack's struggle for survival. Unlike the physical threats the wolves had faced before, this new enemy was a shadow—an elusive force that seemed to appear and disappear without warning, striking fear into the hearts of even the bravest among them. The pack had always been formidable, united under the Alpha's leadership, but the Phantom in the Night had no face, no clear form. It was a presence, a predator that seemed to thrive in the darkness, leaving only fear and destruction in its wake. The Dark Hunter did not fight with the physical strength of other creatures. It fought with terror, with the ability to strike without warning, to slip through the wolves' defenses and disappear before they could retaliate.

The pack had dealt with intruders before—beasts that sought to claim their territory, rivals that wished to challenge their strength. But this was different. The Dark Hunter was not just an invader. It was a relentless force that seemed to prey on their deepest fears. It had no mercy, no negotiation, and no desire for territory. It sought only to hunt, to stalk the wolves from the shadows, striking when they were most vulnerable. Each night, the pack would listen to the winds, the quiet rustle of leaves, the distant sounds of the forest.

And each night, they feared that the Dark Hunter would come. No one knew who—or what—this enemy truly was, but they all knew that its presence was a growing threat that could tear apart their unity.

Tracking the shadows became the pack's obsession. Every wolf, young and old, trained their senses on the smallest signs, hoping for a glimpse of the hunter before it struck again. They searched the forest, looking for the slightest trace of the Phantom's movements—broken branches, disturbed soil, the faintest whisper of an unseen presence. But the Dark Hunter was elusive. It was a master of its domain, operating in the quiet, the darkness, and the space between their most confident moments. The pack had always been the hunters, but now, they found themselves hunted. They were being pushed to their limits, and the only way forward was to confront this shadow head-on, to learn its ways and stop it before it consumed them entirely. The fight for survival was no longer about strength or numbers; it was about resilience, wit, and the courage to face an enemy that could not be seen, only felt.

The Phantom in the Night

The Phantom in the Night was unlike any enemy the pack had ever faced. It wasn't a creature of flesh and blood, but rather a force of fear and uncertainty. The wolves, who had always been the apex predators in their territory, had come to rely on their keen senses—sight, sound, and smell—to navigate the world. But this enemy did not abide by those rules. The Phantom moved in silence, blending seamlessly with the darkness, evading detection with a skill that was beyond anything the wolves had ever encountered. There were no sounds to warn them, no traces left behind to follow. It was as though the very night itself had taken on a form of its own, stalking the pack with a cold, relentless intent.

The first signs of the Phantom's presence were subtle, easily dismissed as the usual disturbances of the forest. A faint rustle in the underbrush, a fleeting shadow that could have been a trick of the light, the sudden stillness in the air. But these small anomalies began to pile up, creating a sense of unease among the wolves. It wasn't until one of the pack members disappeared during a night hunt that the true horror of the Phantom became apparent. The wolves returned to their den at dawn, their senses alert and ready to rest after the hunt, but they found no trace of the missing wolf. No blood, no scent, no signs of struggle. It was as if the wolf had simply vanished into thin air. This eerie disappearance was the first indication that something far more sinister was at play. There were no signs of a fight or an attack, just a vacancy where the pack member had once been.

As the days passed, more wolves began to vanish. The pack's once secure and familiar territory was now a place of growing fear. They would wake up to find their numbers fewer, the space around them increasingly hollow. At first, the Alpha called for caution, directing the pack to be more vigilant, but the disappearance of one wolf after another could not be explained away by simply being careless or unlucky. This was something far more terrifying, and the wolves' spirits began to falter.

The Phantom itself was elusive, never making its presence known in a way that could be pinned down. The wolves tried to track it, moving silently through the woods, searching for any signs of where it might be hiding, but they never found anything. Not a trace of its footsteps, not a hint of its scent. There were nights when the pack would catch a glimpse of something just beyond the treeline—faint shadows flitting between the trunks of trees, a dark silhouette moving faster than any wolf could. But by the time they turned to face it, whatever it was would be gone, leaving only the disquieting silence behind. It was as though the Phantom knew exactly when to appear and when to disappear. It toyed with them, letting them catch only fleeting glimpses of its presence, and then vanishing before they could mount any real response.

The pack's response to this growing terror was a mix of fear and disbelief. They had faced many dangers—rivals from other packs, predators, and the harshness of the wild. They had learned to fight, to adapt, and to protect their own. But this was different. This was something intangible, something that defied their understanding of the world. The wolves had always been creatures of instinct and senses. Their strength lay in their unity, their ability to act as one, to rely on the pack's combined strength to protect and defend. But the Phantom was not a force they could see or fight in the traditional sense. It existed in the gaps—the space between the known and the unknown, in the silence that followed the rustling of leaves, in the shadows that moved where there should have been none.

As the fear mounted, the pack began to unravel. The unity that had always been their greatest strength started to erode. The older wolves, who had weathered countless battles, grew restless. They started questioning their leadership, the Alpha's decisions. Why hadn't they found the Phantom yet? Why hadn't they discovered its weaknesses? The younger wolves, too, began to voice their frustrations. They wanted action, wanted to strike back at the mysterious enemy, but the Alpha held them back. They understood the gravity of the situation—rushing into a confrontation without understanding the nature of the threat would only result in more loss. But in the face of growing panic and a palpable sense of helplessness, the Alpha's words no longer carried the same weight.

The pack's morale faltered further when the next wolf disappeared without a trace. The night had been clear, without a cloud in the sky. The pack had made their way to the hunting grounds, but only a few returned. The scent of the missing wolf was all around, but it ended abruptly, as if the earth had swallowed them whole. There was no sign of a struggle, no sign of an attack. It was as if the very ground had consumed the wolf, leaving nothing behind. It became clear that the Phantom was no mere predator—it was a creature that hunted not with fangs or claws, but with fear and stealth, a predator that played a long, slow game with the wolves' minds.

Days stretched into weeks, and the pack became more and more fractured. They began to look over their shoulders, their senses heightened, waiting for the Phantom to strike again. The atmosphere around them became tense and distrustful. Every noise, every slight movement was met with suspicion. The once-secure den now felt like a trap, the shadows more menacing, the night longer and colder. The wolves began to question the very ground beneath their paws. The Phantom had stolen their peace, their confidence, and now it threatened to steal their unity as well.

The Alpha, however, refused to let the pack fall apart. Even as doubt crept into their mind, the Alpha reminded them that fear alone would not defeat the Phantom. They called the pack together, urging them to remain calm, to trust in each other and their strength. But deep inside, the Alpha knew that this battle was not one they could fight with their usual tactics. This was a battle against something intangible, something that preyed not just on the body, but on the spirit. And the more the pack lost their confidence, the easier it would be for the Phantom to strike again.

It was then that the Alpha realized that the Phantom in the Night was more than just a hunter—it was a test. A test of the pack's resilience, of their ability to remain united in the face of an enemy they could not see. The Phantom thrived on the wolves' fear, growing stronger with every shadow of doubt that took root within them. The only way to fight this enemy, the Alpha understood, was not with force, but with the power of their unity, their ability to trust one another in the face of uncertainty. The pack had to face the Phantom, not as individuals, but as one. Only together could they defeat the darkness that threatened to consume them all.

And so, they set their plan in motion, aware that the Phantom was not just hunting them—it was testing them. The pack had to rise above the fear, above the uncertainty, and confront the shadow that had haunted them for so long. The Phantom in the Night may have been elusive, but the wolves would no longer be its prey. It was time to hunt the hunter.

An Enemy Without Mercy

An Enemy Without Mercy was a force unlike any the pack had ever encountered. Where they had once thrived on the certainty of their strength and the protection of their unity, they now found themselves at the mercy of a predator who felt no obligation to show mercy. The Phantom, the Dark Hunter, had revealed itself to be more than just a lurking threat—it was a cold, calculating force that showed no compassion, no hesitation, and no remorse. This enemy hunted for sport, for dominance, and most chillingly, for the destruction of the pack itself.

Unlike the other predators the pack had faced, the Dark Hunter did not operate with instinct alone. It did not fight for survival or for food, nor did it strike in the heat of the moment. It was precise and methodical, acting with a cruel intelligence that made it even more dangerous. Its every move was calculated to break the wolves' spirit. The wolves could not comprehend the sheer coldness of this enemy. There was no negotiation, no compromise, no desire for anything other than their complete annihilation. The Dark Hunter's objective was clear: to tear apart the pack by any means necessary, and to do so in a way that left nothing but destruction in its wake.

From the very first encounter, the wolves knew they were up against something different. The pack had always prided itself on its ability to fight and defend with brutal efficiency. They had faced larger, stronger opponents before, and they had always emerged victorious through sheer determination and unity. But the Dark Hunter's approach was unlike any they had encountered. It struck from the shadows, often unseen, leaving no traces of its presence except the growing unease among the wolves. It was as though the very air around them had thickened with its malevolent presence.

The pack began to feel the weight of this invisible predator pressing down on them. Their instincts told them to be alert, to stay together, but the unpredictability of the Dark Hunter made it impossible to form any reliable defense. It attacked when least expected, sowing confusion and fear, and then disappeared before the wolves could mount any counterattack. The wounds it left were not always physical; often, they were psychological. The mere presence of the Dark Hunter was enough to paralyze the pack with dread. Even the Alpha, once unwavering and confident, began to question how they could lead a pack when the enemy was not something they could see or touch.

It was clear that the Dark Hunter's method was to disorient and dismantle the pack's cohesion. It knew how to manipulate fear, to fracture the wolves' unity and to make them doubt their strength. The pack, once united, now found themselves turning on one another. The older wolves grew more protective, urging the younger members to stay in the center of the group, while the younger wolves began to grow frustrated, feeling their strength being wasted in the face of an enemy that could not be defeated by brute force alone. Tensions began to rise. The trust that had always held the pack together began to erode, and fear began to replace the confidence they had once taken for granted. The Dark Hunter had not just attacked them physically—it was now attacking their sense of purpose and identity.

The Alpha, though deeply troubled, understood the game the Dark Hunter was playing. The enemy was trying to tear apart their cohesion by exploiting their fear. They could not afford to let the pack splinter. They needed to bring the wolves back together, to remind them of what they were fighting for. The Dark Hunter could take lives, could strike from the shadows, but it could never destroy the bond between the wolves if they remained united.

But unity, in this case, was difficult to achieve. Every day the pack lived under the shadow of this unseen enemy, they began to lose something more than their confidence—they lost their hope. The constant fear gnawed at them, making them question their ability to defend themselves. They had always been the predators, the ones who could track and hunt with precision, but now they were the hunted, driven into hiding by a foe who knew how to manipulate the landscape, the weather, and the pack's own fears to its advantage.

The turning point came when the pack, having spent days avoiding the Dark Hunter, finally confronted the reality that their traditional methods of survival were no longer enough. The wolves were skilled hunters, but they had never faced an adversary that could not be caught or fought in a straightforward battle. They had to adapt, had to rethink their strategy, or they would be driven to extinction by the Dark Hunter's unrelenting pursuit.

The Alpha called a meeting, a final attempt to rally the pack. The wolves gathered, their faces drawn and weary. The weight of the past weeks had taken its toll on them, but the Alpha knew they could not afford to let the pack lose hope entirely. They reminded the wolves of their shared strength, their shared history, and the bonds that had held them together for so long. The Dark Hunter, despite its ruthlessness, was still just a single entity. It could not destroy them unless they allowed it. The Alpha's words were calm but fierce, a quiet resolve in their voice. "We are not just wolves. We are a pack. And as long as we stand together, no enemy—no matter how relentless—can break us."

In that moment, something shifted within the pack. The fear that had paralyzed them began to recede, replaced by a spark of defiance. The wolves were still afraid—how could they not be, facing an enemy that operated in shadows? But they were also united, and that unity was their greatest weapon. They could not fight the Dark Hunter on its terms, in the shadows, but they could turn the tables. They could use the hunter's own tactics against it, striking from unexpected places, making the enemy doubt its own power.

The pack began to hunt together again, but this time, they did not chase blindly. They moved as a coordinated unit, their movements calculated and purposeful. They used the cover of darkness to their advantage, setting traps and creating diversions. The Dark Hunter, for the first time, began to feel the pressure of a united pack that would not yield to fear. The wolves learned to fight in the shadows as well, using stealth and subterfuge to keep the enemy on the defensive. Each small victory against the Dark Hunter, each time they outwitted it, brought back a small piece of the confidence they had lost.

However, the battle was not won easily, nor would it be quickly. The Dark Hunter was relentless, always slipping just out of reach, always waiting for the moment when the wolves would falter. But in that pursuit, the wolves learned something invaluable—that an enemy without mercy could still be defeated, not through brute force, but through patience, intelligence, and the power of unity. The Dark Hunter had underestimated them. It had believed that fear could break them, but it had underestimated the wolves' ability to adapt, to evolve, and to fight for each other.

As the days passed and the pack became more skilled in their counterattacks, the balance began to shift. The Dark Hunter, though still a threat, was no longer invincible. The pack had found their strength again, not by overpowering the hunter, but by learning to live with it, to outthink it, and to remain united in the face of its terror. The Phantom in the Night had not broken them, and they were determined that it never would.

Tracking the Shadows

Tracking the Shadows became the pack's obsession, their only chance to reclaim the safety and security they had lost. The Dark Hunter, a phantom of the night, had eluded them for so long that the wolves could no longer afford to react out of fear alone. They had been cornered, scattered, and manipulated by the relentless terror that the Phantom instilled in their hearts. But now, something had shifted within the pack. They could no longer wait passively for the Hunter to strike again. They had to take the fight to the shadows, to track the elusive enemy, and make it pay for the suffering it had caused.

The first step in tracking the shadows was to understand how the Dark Hunter operated. The pack had always relied on their instincts, on their connection to the land, and on their ability to read the environment. But this new enemy defied the very principles they had honed over generations. The Dark Hunter did not leave behind the obvious signs that they were accustomed to finding—broken branches, claw marks on trees, or scent trails that could be followed. The Phantom moved in ways that made it almost impossible to predict, and when it struck, it left no trace of its presence.

The Alpha, frustrated by their inability to track the Phantom, called for a strategy meeting. The pack, feeling the weight of the situation, gathered in the safety of their den, their bodies tense with the shared anxiety of being hunted. The Alpha stood before them, their voice low but commanding. "We cannot afford to be the prey any longer," they said. "We have faced many threats before, but this is different. We cannot fight what we cannot see. We must become the hunters, not just in the physical world, but in the world of the mind. We will learn to track the shadows, and we will use the darkness to our advantage."

The Alpha's words were not just a call to action—they were a reminder of what the pack was capable of. They had faced down enemies larger and more powerful than themselves, had survived in a world that demanded constant vigilance. But to track the Dark Hunter, they would have to shift their thinking. They would need to become more than just predators of the forest; they would have to become predators of the mind, able to think and act in ways the Dark Hunter could not anticipate.

The pack began their new training with a focus on perception. They started to watch for the smallest disturbances in their environment—shifting shadows, the movement of the wind, the flicker of an unfamiliar form at the edge of their vision. They spent long hours moving through the forest, using every trick they knew to sharpen their senses and heighten their awareness. The wolves trained in silence, learning to communicate without words, relying solely on body language and subtle gestures. The goal was to become so attuned to their surroundings that even the smallest hint of the Phantom's presence would not go unnoticed.

Days turned into weeks as the pack practiced relentlessly, and slowly, they began to notice patterns in the darkness. While the Dark Hunter was masterful at remaining hidden, there were certain things that even it could not control. The wolves began to track the temperature of the air, the displacement of dust and leaves, the faintest sound in the night that didn't quite match the usual rhythm of the forest. They learned to listen for the telltale silence that followed the Phantom's passage—a silence that could be felt as much as it was heard. The lack of sound, the absence of life, was the Phantom's calling card. It was the moment of its approach, and the wolves began to use this knowledge to their advantage.

The pack also learned to work in tandem. They knew that alone, they were vulnerable, but together, they were stronger than any one wolf. They began to take turns monitoring the perimeter of their territory, working in pairs to increase their chances of spotting the Phantom. One wolf would remain still and watch for any sign of movement, while the other would remain hidden, using the cover of darkness to scout for any disturbances. It was a delicate balance of patience and alertness. They had to remain focused for hours, sometimes days, as the Phantom seemed to grow more elusive with every passing night.

The Alpha, too, was deeply invested in this new approach. They had always been the leader, the one to guide the pack through difficult times, but they now understood that their role had changed. They could no longer be the solitary protector—they had to be part of the team, sharing the burden of tracking the hunter. Together, they began to map out the Phantom's movements, studying the ground for any sign of disturbance. They observed the natural world around them more closely, watching the behavior of the other creatures in the forest. If the Phantom was moving through the trees, it would affect the normal flow of life. The birds would go quiet, the smaller animals would retreat into the shadows, and even the wind would shift as if it too were disturbed by the presence of this dark force.

One night, after weeks of carefully watching and waiting, they finally saw something. It was a flicker at the edge of the trees, a shadow that didn't belong. The pack had been in position for hours, waiting for the slightest hint of movement, and now, at last, they saw it. The Phantom had moved into their territory again, just as they had anticipated. But this time, the pack was ready. They had practiced the art of patience, of remaining still and silent, and now they were prepared to make their move.

The Alpha signaled the pack to move. They had learned that the key to tracking the shadows was not rushing forward blindly, but to be patient, to move slowly and deliberately. The wolves spread out, staying low to the ground, their movements synchronized in a way that made them invisible to the Phantom. They moved through the forest like whispers on the wind, their eyes constantly scanning for any movement in the darkness.

Finally, they closed in on the figure they had been tracking for so long. The Phantom, though elusive, had not anticipated such a coordinated effort. The wolves, using the very shadows the Phantom had relied on, were now able to anticipate its next move. It was a moment of triumph, but it was also a moment of realization. The Phantom was not invincible. It could be tracked, it could be caught, and it could be defeated—not through brute force, but through the cunning and unity of the pack.

But as the pack prepared to strike, they knew this was not the end of the Dark Hunter's presence. The Phantom had only revealed itself because it had underestimated them. There was no victory in this first encounter, only a temporary shift in the balance. The pack understood that their fight against the Phantom was not just a battle of strength, but a battle of endurance, intelligence, and unity. The darkness would always be a part of their world, but they had learned how to move within it, how to track it, and how to use it to their advantage.

Tracking the Shadows had become more than just a strategy—it had become the wolves' new way of life. They would no longer be prey to fear and uncertainty. Together, they would hunt the shadows and take back what had been stolen from them. The Phantom was not their end—it was their beginning.

Chapter 10
The Final Stand

The Final Stand was fast approaching, and the air was thick with tension. After months of being hunted and tested by unseen forces, the pack found themselves at a crossroads. The time for subtlety and evasion had passed. The Dark Hunter, the Phantom in the Night, and all the threats that had been closing in on them now demanded a decisive response. The pack, once fractured by fear and distrust, now stood united by the shared understanding that their survival depended on one thing: standing together, no matter the cost. The Alpha had spent countless nights trying to hold the pack together, guiding them through the darkness. Now, they were no longer just defending their territory—they were fighting for their very existence.

The Gathering Storm had been brewing for weeks. The intruders, once a distant concern, had now made their presence known. The pack had learned to track the shadows, but even their sharp senses could not predict the full extent of the danger that was about to unfold. The Dark Hunter was no longer just a terror lurking in the dark; it had become the symbol of all their struggles. Every wolf knew that the upcoming battle would not just be against a singular enemy, but against everything that had threatened their unity, their strength, and their legacy.

Preparing for Battle was a grueling task. The wolves had trained their bodies and minds for this moment, but the fight ahead was unlike any they had faced. The terrain would be unforgiving, and their enemies were relentless. They had lost wolves in the shadows, suffered betrayals, and been pushed to their limits. But in the face of this overwhelming threat, they found their strength in one another. The Alpha, though weighed down by the responsibility of leadership, drew from the unity that had begun to heal. Together, they would face whatever came, not as individuals, but as a pack, bound by blood, fur, and shared purpose.

The Clash of Fangs and Steel would mark the culmination of everything the pack had endured. It would be the ultimate test of their resilience, their bond, and their will to survive. The fate of the pack would be decided in that final confrontation—an all-out battle where survival was uncertain, and every wolf would have to fight not just for themselves, but for the pack that had always stood beside them.

The Gathering Storm

The Gathering Storm was not just a storm of nature, but a storm of fate—an impending clash that loomed over the pack, a dark, ominous force that they could not outrun. The signs had been there for weeks, subtle at first, barely noticeable, but they grew more undeniable with each passing day. Tensions within the pack had reached a boiling point, and the external threats—the Phantom in the Night, the Dark Hunter, and the intruders—had become a constant presence, pushing the wolves into a corner. The forest, once their sanctuary, had become a place of danger, where each rustle of leaves and every shadow held the potential for catastrophe.

For the pack, it was clear: they were on the brink of something far greater than any battle they had fought before. The external dangers had always been there, but the constant threat from within—the fracture in their unity, the loss of trust, and the betrayal—had left them weakened. The strength that had once bound them together was now brittle, cracked by doubt and fear. The alpha's attempts to bring the pack together had met with limited success; though the younger wolves had finally accepted the need for unity, there was a sense that something was missing. The pack was not as strong as it once had been, and they could feel it.

But in the face of this, they had no choice but to stand together. The storm that was gathering in the distance would not wait for them to heal. The time for hesitation was over. The wolves could no longer afford to question their loyalty to each other. The Dark Hunter had hunted them in the shadows for too long, and the intruders had pushed into their territory with growing force. Every wolf knew that the moment had come to face the storm, to take a stand, or risk losing everything.

The Alpha stood at the forefront of the gathering storm, watching the skies darken with the weight of impending conflict. There was no longer any room for uncertainty. They had learned to track the Phantom, but now the time had come for a different kind of preparation. The pack needed to be united, not just in body, but in spirit. The Alpha understood that the wolves would need more than just physical strength to survive this fight—they needed the strength of their bonds, the trust that had once been the core of their unity. But even as the Alpha called for unity, they could feel the storm brewing inside them as well. They had always been the protector, the one who held the pack together, but in this moment, they knew that even their leadership could not guarantee victory.

The pack had to find its strength within, not just follow the lead of one wolf. Each member had to believe in the fight ahead.

The younger wolves, fueled by impatience and fear, began to prepare themselves with the same fervor that had marked their previous hunts. They were eager for action, eager to prove themselves in the face of this unknown enemy. But their eagerness was tempered by the knowledge that the enemy they faced was unlike any they had hunted before. The Dark Hunter, the Phantom, was no simple predator. It was a force that preyed not just on the body, but on the mind and spirit. To fight this enemy, the younger wolves would need more than just raw power—they would need discipline, patience, and the understanding that victory was not guaranteed.

The older wolves, wiser and more measured, began preparing in their own way. They knew that the strength of the pack lay not in any one individual's actions but in their collective effort. The older wolves worked with the younger ones, teaching them how to stay calm in the face of uncertainty, how to trust each other even when fear threatened to overwhelm them. They reminded the younger wolves that the storm that was gathering outside would only be overcome if they stayed true to the unity that had always been their greatest strength. As much as the older wolves wanted to lead the charge, they knew that this battle would be won by the pack as a whole, not by any single wolf.

The storm that gathered in the distance mirrored the storm that brewed within the pack itself. The Alpha understood that the greatest danger they faced was not the enemy that stalked them in the shadows, but the division within their own ranks. The betrayal they had suffered had left scars, deep and painful, and they had yet to fully heal. The pack had to confront its own wounds before it could face the external enemy. The Alpha gathered the wolves in a final, desperate attempt to unite them, to remind them of what they had always fought for. The words were spoken not as a command, but as a plea—one last chance to restore the unity that was so critical to their survival.

The Alpha's voice rang out through the gathering pack. "We face a storm, but we do not face it alone. We have always been strong, not because of any one wolf, but because we have fought together, side by side, in the face of every challenge. We will fight this battle together, or we will fall apart. But I believe in each and every one of you. I believe in our pack."

The wolves, despite the growing tension, began to feel the weight of those words. The storm outside might be coming, but so too was their strength. They knew the Dark Hunter was a merciless enemy, but they also knew that they had faced the impossible before. Together, they had overcome every obstacle the forest had thrown their way, and though this storm felt different, they would stand as one to face it. The pack was united again—not just by the Alpha's command, but by their own shared determination to protect what was theirs.

The gathering storm did not just represent the external threat. It represented everything the pack had struggled with in the last months—the fear, the division, the doubt. But now, as the Alpha spoke, the storm began to feel like something they could control, something they could face and overcome together. They understood now that the greatest weapon they had was not the strength of their jaws or their claws, but the bond that tied them all together. The storm might rage, but they would face it as a unified force.

As the wolves prepared for the battle ahead, the weight of the gathering storm was heavy in the air, but so too was the unspoken resolve. They would not let this storm destroy them. The time for hesitation had passed, and now they stood ready. The wolves knew that the path ahead would not be easy, that the storm would challenge them in ways they had never imagined. But they also knew that they would face it as one. The pack would rise or fall together, and the strength of their unity would be the key to surviving the dark days that lay ahead. The gathering storm was upon them—but so was their courage.

Preparing for Battle

Preparing for Battle was a task that went beyond just sharpening claws and honing skills. It was a mental, emotional, and spiritual preparation, one that demanded total unity and focus. The wolves, once united by instinct and shared history, now had to consciously decide to unite in purpose. The coming battle was unlike any they had ever faced. The enemy they were preparing to confront, whether it was the Phantom in the Night or the intruders at their gates, was not a force they could take lightly. They would need more than just strength; they would need the courage to face the unknown, the resilience to endure pain, and the clarity to make the right choices when the battle began.

The Alpha called the pack together in the clearing, the darkened sky above them a grim reminder that the battle would not wait. Every wolf, from the youngest pup to the oldest warrior, stood in silence, their eyes reflecting the weight of the moment. The atmosphere was thick with tension, and yet, there was a sense of purpose. They had been tested before, but now they were on the cusp of something more dangerous. The Alpha, standing at the front of the gathering, spoke with authority and a quiet desperation. "This battle will not just be fought with fangs and claws. It will be fought with our unity, with our strength of spirit. We will face the darkness together, or we will fall apart alone."

The Alpha's words were not just a rallying cry—they were a reminder of what was at stake. The pack had fought many battles before, but none like this. The enemies they faced were not just physical threats. The Dark Hunter, with its uncanny ability to strike from the shadows, the Phantom in the Night who hunted not for food but for fear—these were not enemies that could be easily defeated. The wolves understood that they needed to think differently. This battle would not be about brute force; it would be about outsmarting the enemy, about turning the very forces of fear against them.

The preparation began with an assessment of the pack's strengths and weaknesses. The Alpha, always focused on strategy, gathered the older wolves and the warriors to discuss their battle plans. They knew that the only way they could win was to capitalize on their strengths while covering their weaknesses. Each wolf had their role to play, and each one had to be ready for whatever came. The younger wolves, eager to prove themselves, were assigned tasks that required speed and agility. They would be the scouts, the ones who moved swiftly through the trees, searching for any sign of the enemy. Their job was to observe, to gather intelligence, and to remain undetected. The older wolves, experienced and steady, were tasked with the more direct approach—defending the pack, securing their territory, and ensuring that the pack could not be cornered. They were the foundation of the defense, the ones who would stand firm when the battle raged.

The pack spent hours each day preparing for the inevitable clash. They honed their skills, practiced hunting together, and strengthened their coordination. The training was grueling, as the wolves pushed themselves to their limits. Every movement, every shift in position, had to be perfect. They had to be faster, smarter, and more adaptable than their enemy. The forest, once a place of comfort, now felt like a battleground. They moved through it with heightened senses, each wolf learning to move with more precision, to detect even the faintest signs of their unseen enemies.

One of the most important aspects of their preparation was mental and emotional fortitude. The Alpha gathered the pack for one final meeting before the battle, urging them to prepare not just their bodies but their minds. "Fear will be our greatest enemy in this battle," the Alpha said. "The Dark Hunter and the Phantom in the Night seek to break us through fear. We will not let them. We will face the darkness with the strength of the pack. Remember, we fight not just for survival, but for each other."

These words resonated deeply with the pack. The wolves were no longer just individuals fighting for themselves. They were a collective, a unit that thrived on loyalty, trust, and shared purpose. They had always fought for the survival of the pack as a whole, but now the stakes were even higher. Their unity would be their greatest strength, and they had to remind themselves of this, especially when the pressure became unbearable.

The preparations were not just physical and emotional, but spiritual. The pack needed to tap into something deeper than just their desire to survive. They needed to remember why they fought—not just for territory, not just for the pack's survival, but for the bond they shared with one another and with the land they called home. The Alpha, with the help of the older wolves, led a ceremony under the moonlight, where each wolf reaffirmed their connection to the pack. The ceremony was simple, but powerful. It was a reminder of the strength that came from their unity, of the blood and fur that tied them together, and of the ancestors who had fought before them.

The night before the battle, the pack rested, though sleep was elusive. There was a quiet sense of anticipation in the air, a realization that this was the moment they had been preparing for. The forest around them was eerily silent, as if holding its breath. The usual sounds of the forest were muted, and the wolves could feel the weight of the impending conflict pressing down on them. But despite the uncertainty, they stood together. They had prepared as best as they could, and now they would face the storm.

The Alpha, ever the leader, walked among the pack that night, offering a quiet word of encouragement to each wolf. It wasn't just the younger wolves who needed reassurance; even the older wolves, who had fought many battles, needed to feel the strength of their bond. "Remember why we fight," the Alpha said softly to the wolves around them. "We fight for each other. We fight for our home. And we fight for the future of the pack."

The moment of battle was fast approaching. The winds had shifted, and the forest felt charged with energy. The pack was ready—mentally, physically, and emotionally. The battle that awaited them would not be one of sheer strength, but one of strategy, unity, and resilience. They had faced the shadows and had learned to track them. They had faced betrayal and had learned to rebuild trust. Now, they would face their greatest test yet, but they were no longer afraid. Together, they would stand against the darkness and fight with everything they had.

As the Alpha looked out over the pack, they knew that no matter what the outcome, they had prepared to the best of their ability. They were not just wolves anymore. They were a force, a family, and nothing could tear them apart. The battle would be fierce, but they were ready. The pack was united, and together, they would face whatever came their way. The storm had gathered, and now, it was time to fight.

The Clash of Fangs and Steel

The Clash of Fangs and Steel was a battle that would define the pack's future, one that would test their very existence and their ability to survive in a world where darkness and fear threatened to swallow them whole. The storm that had been building for weeks had finally reached its peak, and the pack was no longer waiting for the enemy to make its move. The time for hesitation was over. The wolves had prepared as best as they could—mentally, emotionally, and physically. Now, they were ready to face the enemy head-on.

As dawn broke over the horizon, the forest felt charged with anticipation. The usual morning sounds—the chirping of birds, the rustling of leaves—seemed muffled by the oppressive weight of what was to come. The pack moved in formation, their bodies tensed and alert, their senses heightened by the knowledge that this would be a fight to the death. The Alpha led them with quiet confidence, their eyes scanning the trees, ears flicking at every sound. They had faced many battles in their lifetime, but this one felt different—this was not just about defending territory. It was about survival.

The enemy they faced had no mercy, no desire for anything but destruction. The Dark Hunter, a phantom who had stalked them from the shadows, and the intruders, a foreign force that threatened to claim what was rightfully theirs, were about to converge on the pack's heart. The wolves had trained for this moment, but now that it was here, there was no turning back. Every wolf knew that the battle ahead would not be fought with just strength, but with strategy and unity. This was not the time for individual heroics; it was the time to fight as a single, unified force.

The wolves moved through the forest like shadows, their bodies low to the ground, every step measured. The younger wolves, eager for battle, were filled with a mixture of fear and determination. The older wolves, experienced and steady, were more cautious, their eyes sharp, watching every movement, listening for any hint of the enemy's approach. They had seen enough battle to know that the first strike would be crucial, and they couldn't afford to make a mistake.

The Alpha signaled for the wolves to halt, their body still, listening. In the distance, the faintest sound of movement reached their ears. The enemy was close. The Alpha gave a low, sharp growl, signaling for the pack to spread out, each wolf taking their position. The plan was simple: they would surround the enemy, using their knowledge of the terrain to their advantage. The wolves knew the land better than anyone, and they intended to use the forest itself as a weapon. The battle would be fought in the shadows, where the Dark Hunter thrived, and the pack would use their own stealth to outmaneuver the enemy.

Suddenly, the stillness was shattered by the first sound of conflict—a brutal clash of fangs and claws as the wolves and the intruders collided in a savage rush. The sound of battle echoed through the trees as the pack fought tooth and claw, each wolf engaging with their opponent in a deadly dance of survival. The younger wolves, quick and agile, darted between the trees, using their speed to strike at the intruders from unexpected angles. They were fierce, their youthful energy propelling them into the fray with a hunger for victory. But they had yet to face the full force of their enemies.

The older wolves, slower but far more experienced, held their ground, defending the perimeter and making sure the younger wolves had room to maneuver. They fought with calculated precision, using their strength and endurance to wear down their foes. Their fangs sank deep into the flesh of the intruders, but they also knew when to pull back and regroup, a tactical advantage that came from years of experience in the wild.

The Dark Hunter, though elusive and hard to track, was not absent from the battle. It moved through the trees like a shadow, striking with silent precision. The pack had learned to anticipate its movements, but the Phantom's ability to blend into the darkness made it a dangerous foe. The Alpha, ever alert, kept their senses trained on the shifting shadows, watching for any sign of the hunter's approach. They knew that the true challenge of this battle would not come from the intruders but from the unseen predator that had plagued them for so long.

The wolves fought with everything they had, their hearts filled with the determination to protect their home and their pack. The ground was soon littered with fallen leaves, broken branches, and the sounds of struggle. Blood was spilled, and the air was thick with the scent of the battle. The pack fought with ferocity, but they also fought with heart, knowing that each blow they landed, each strike they delivered, was for the pack's survival.

The Alpha, sensing the battle had reached its peak, rallied the wolves with a powerful howl. The sound ripped through the forest, a cry of defiance that echoed across the trees. It was a call to arms, a rallying cry for the pack to fight as one. The pack responded with their own howls, their voices rising in unison, each wolf reaffirming their loyalty to the Alpha and to one another. The sound of their united howls was a powerful force in itself, a declaration that they would not fall, that they would not be driven from their land.

But the battle was far from over. The Dark Hunter, ever patient, struck again, taking down one of the younger wolves with a swift and silent attack. The wolf, though strong, had been caught off guard. The pack's unity faltered for a moment as fear swept through them. The young wolf was down, and they could hear its desperate cries, but they also knew that they couldn't stop now. They had to keep moving, keep fighting, or they would lose everything.

The Alpha, their heart heavy with the loss, pushed forward, leading the charge with renewed intensity. They would not let the sacrifice of one wolf be in vain. The pack closed ranks, their movements synchronized in a way that only wolves who had fought together for years could achieve. They fought not just for the land, but for each other. With each blow they struck, with each foe they felled, the pack's unity grew stronger. They were no longer just a group of wolves—they were a single force, an unstoppable entity driven by their shared love for the pack.

The battle raged on for what felt like an eternity. The air was thick with the scent of blood, the ground stained by the conflict. But slowly, the intruders began to retreat. The wolves' resilience had worn them down, and the Dark Hunter, though still lurking in the shadows, could not stop the tide of battle. The pack had found their strength again, and with one final push, they overwhelmed the enemy.

As the dust settled and the wolves stood victorious, their bodies bruised and bloodied, they looked around at the battlefield. The cost of the fight had been high. The pack had lost members, and their territory had been scarred. But they had survived. They had fought as one, and they had won. The Dark Hunter, though still out there, had been forced back into the shadows, unable to break their spirit.

The pack stood together, their breathing heavy, their eyes locked in silent understanding. They had faced the storm, and though they had emerged battered, they had emerged together. The Clash of Fangs and Steel had tested them, but it had also proven something crucial—they were stronger than any force that sought to destroy them. Together, they would rebuild, heal, and face whatever new challenges the future would bring. But for now, they were united in their victory.

Conclusion

In the end, the wolves emerged from the storm of battle scarred, yet stronger than ever before. The pack had faced the greatest challenge of their existence—an enemy unlike any they had encountered, an enemy that preyed on their fears, their unity, and their very existence. But through it all, they had proven something vital: that their strength was not just in their claws or teeth, but in the bond they shared. This was the true victory—one of unity, resilience, and the power of trust.

The Alpha, though weary, stood proud as they looked upon their pack. The land had been ravaged by the battle, but life began to return. The forests once again became a place of safety, where the wolves could roam freely, knowing that they had reclaimed their territory. The bond between them, however, was the most significant thing they had won. They had come to realize that survival was not merely about strength—it was about standing together, shoulder to shoulder, no matter what the world threw at them.

The younger wolves, who had once been driven by impatience and the desire to prove themselves, now understood the true meaning of leadership and survival. They had witnessed the price of blind ambition and learned the importance of patience, strategy, and trust. Their hunger for action had been tempered by the harsh realities of the battle, and they now knew that the strength of the pack lay in more than just their youthful energy. It lay in the lessons passed down from the older wolves, in the quiet wisdom that came with experience.

The older wolves, who had long carried the weight of the pack's traditions, felt a renewed sense of hope. They had seen their way of life challenged, their unity questioned, but they had also witnessed the younger generation step up in ways they had never imagined. The strength of the pack was no longer just in the paws of the old, but in the hearts of the new. They knew that the future of the pack was in capable paws, and that the legacy of their ancestors would endure.

The Alpha, looking at the wolves they had led through so many trials, realized that leadership had never been about commanding from the front—it had been about knowing when to step back and let the pack lead themselves. They had survived not because the Alpha had been strong, but because the pack had been united, and because every wolf had played their part in the battle. The Alpha's role was not to fight for them, but to guide them, to remind them of the strength they had when they stood together.

As the pack gathered around the Alpha, they felt the bond that had once seemed so fragile growing stronger. The memories of the battle, the losses they had suffered, and the fear they had overcome, were now a part of their shared history. They knew that their fight was never just about surviving in the wild—it was about protecting each other, holding onto what mattered, and ensuring that the pack would endure for generations to come.

The wolves were no longer the same. They had faced their greatest trial, and though the scars would remain, they had learned invaluable lessons. They had learned that the greatest strength was found not in the fangs and claws, but in the unity that held them together. They had learned that even in the darkest moments, when fear seemed to consume them, they could stand tall, shoulder to shoulder, and face the storm together.

The story of their survival, of their victory over the darkness, would be passed down through the generations. It was a story not just of survival, but of hope, of the power of unity, and of the unbreakable bond that existed between the pack. The wolves had faced their darkest hour, and they had emerged victorious, stronger, and more united than ever before.

And so, with the storm behind them and the future uncertain, the wolves continued their journey through the forest, knowing that no matter what came next, they would face it as one—united, unbroken, and stronger than ever before. The pack's legacy would live on, a testament to the power of unity and the strength that comes from standing together in the face of adversity. The fight was not over, but the wolves were ready—together, they would face whatever came next.

www.ingramcontent.com/pod-product-compliance
Lightning Source LLC
LaVergne TN
LVHW061554070526
838199LV00077B/7042